Teaching Mathematics

Teaching Mathematics:
Strategies That Work
K-12

Teachers Writing to Teachers Series

**Edited by Mark Driscoll
and Jere Confrey
Assistant editor Elsa Martz**

**Heinemann
Portsmouth, NH**

HEINEMANN EDUCATIONAL BOOKS, INC.
70 Court Street, Portsmouth, NH 03801

London   Edinburgh   Melbourne   Auckland
Hong Kong   Singapore   Kuala Lumpur
New Delhi   Ibadan   Nairobi   Johannesburg
Kingston   Port of Spain

ISBN 0-435-08302-3
Printed and manufactured in the United States of America.
10   9   8   7   6   5   4   3   2   1

CONTENTS

INTRODUCTION

Dozens of books and reports on education have been published in the past few years, and so it is fair to ask the two editors of this book, "Why another?" The first, very practical answer to that question is that its predecessor, **Understanding Writing: Teachers Writing to Teachers,** has been so successful. That book has had an enormous appeal for teachers of writing throughout the country, and has evidently struck the right chords among the thousands of them who have purchased it in the past few years.

The second reason is tied to our recollection of a survey conducted about twenty years ago that astounded many in the field of education with one of its findings. A relatively large number of teachers, it told us, never thought much about **how** children learn. ("Do Teachers Understand Learning Theory?" by C.A. Weber, the **Kappan,** May 1965.) We do not know whether this state of affairs has changed in the intervening years. We do know, however, that teachers who listen to their students and think deeply about how children do and ought to learn mathematics have had few forums in which they could express their opinions. This book was designed to provide such a forum.

We believe that **Understanding Writing** has been appealing to teachers because of its design: teachers writing to teachers. It deviates from the typical outside-expert model of education books. Similarly, we are convinced that the best source of inspiration and growth for a mathematics teacher who is keen on professional growth is another mathematics teacher who is also keen on professional growth, has thought about how children learn mathematics, and who has a new strategy or a different perspective to offer. There is a level of energy and empowerment in this kind of teacher-teacher interaction that no research expert offering his or her opinion can hope to match.

Teacher-teacher interaction is also a vehicle for professional problem solving. In fact, of all the mechanisms that have been or could be applied to the problems besetting mathematics education in this country, one of the least tapped is teachers communicating with teachers. The norm, as Theodore Sizer so graphically depicts in **Horace's Compromise,** is for teachers to become isolated. An elementary school teacher in Michigan, whom we both met in 1983 during a site visit for A Study of Exemplary Mathematics Programs, surprised us when we asked why she thought her school's program was exemplary: "This is the fifth school in which I've taught in this district, and it's the first one in which the teachers share with each other." When we asked what she meant by sharing, she replied, "Share **anything**—ideas, tests, classroom materials, magazine articles."

As we traveled the country a few years ago, visiting exemplary mathematics programs for our study, we were frequently impressed by the sharing and other professional interactions among the programs' mathematics teachers. In various ways, the teachers work together to stay abreast of student needs, to foresee and plan for necessary curriculum revisions, to keep student expectations about learning mathematics high, and so on, through all of the problems and challenges that typically hound mathematics teachers at all grade levels. Since these were programs with records of impressive success in student outcomes, it was easy to infer that the teacher-teacher interactions were affecting, even nourishing, the success. Certainly, the teachers themselves seemed nourished by the interactions, and it is that kind of nourishment that we hope to foster with this book. With its recent renewed support for summer institutes for mathematics and science teachers, the National Science Foundation has given a boost to teacher-teacher interaction. We hope that NSF has started a national trend toward using teacher communication, sharing, and networking to solve common mathematics teaching problems, and that this book can help to move the trend along.

The chapters in this book cover the entire spectrum of grades, from kindergarten to high school and beyond, with topics that also cover a wide range. However, behind the variety are some common threads that bind the teacher-authors together. Most evident is the passion and life they inject into their stories and recommendations for change, which come across as a clear rejection of Horace's isolation. These teachers are eager to pass their ideas for success on to their colleagues.

Also evident in most of these chapters is the underlying realization of the teacher-writers that vibrant mathematics teaching does not live by content alone, that there are psychological and social forces at work in the classroom that should not be ignored. Repeatedly, these teachers write of the importance of **listening to students,** building models of how their students are viewing the ideas and then developing or revising their curriculum to respond to these needs. Perhaps nowhere in this book is the evolution of such a process made more clearly than in the chapter by Susan Larkin as she has her fourth graders write word problems for each other. Jacqueline Simmons and her colleagues describe their experience using paired problem solving where students are encouraged to talk through mathematics with each other, exploring the reasons behind errors and learning to build precision and clarity. Arthur Powell illustrates the use of journal writing as a vehicle in which teachers and students can communicate. In her chapter, Carolyn Reese-Dukes reminds us that students' worlds of learning are also emotional worlds, where their learning is influenced by their feelings about themselves, their mathematical competence, and their levels of success. She urges teachers to reach out and directly address these affective as well as cognitive psychological issues.

The content of the curriculum also is scrutinized by these teacher-authors. Mathematics is portrayed as a lively human activity, not as a static set of truths whose meaning is only available to a select few. This is vividly portrayed in the article by Henry Borenson with his methods for coaching and cajoling young students to think for themselves and defend their thinking. Bernadine Krawczyk's **In Search of the Woozle** illustrates the same point with young children. Her children explore the circle through a variety of activities that appeal to daily experience with circles and roundness through several of the senses.

There are few images in these chapters of students seated working diligently and passively on worksheets and texts. The students are active, using manipulatives and building mathematical ideas, as in Joan McNichols' article about using manipulative materials with young children who have learning difficulties. Older students are equally active in the article by Richard Houde and Michal Yerushalmy wherein they describe the Geometric Supposer, an innovative piece of microcomputer tool software, with which one student has developed an original mathematical theorem. Mona Fabricant, recognizing the potential of software to relieve teachers of the burden of correcting endless stacks of routine problems, describes the virtues and vices of current software. In it, her lessons to software developers and publishers are clear: build software that can be used efficiently by teachers to assist them in their instruction, not to add more obstructions to their task.

The social side of mathematics education—questions such as who gets access to mathematical ideas—is addressed indirectly and directly in a number of articles. Martin Simon's case study, describing a child whose talents would have remained unnoticed under traditional instruction but who showed promise when nurtured, is undeniably significant. Susette Jacquette and Bonnie Mellow describe programs for underachievers and average students, respectively, using laboratory activities which seem to spark interest and personal successes for some of our students who are most at risk—girls, minorities, and underprepared students.

In summary, these chapters have been written by a group of talented and enthusiastic professionals who wanted to write to their colleagues about a pedagogy of mathematics. Their focus is a process consistent with the important factors we noted in our Study of Exemplary Mathematics Programs. In particular, teaching mathematics is portrayed in these pages as:

1. an **active** process, where students are involved in mathematical activities, searching for patterns, categorizing, problem solving, conjecturing, defending, and reflecting;

2. a **negotiated** process, where teachers' expectations for student success are high, where teachers and students each hold responsibility in the system, and where risk-taking on all sides is permitted and supported;

3. a **dedicated** process wherein the teachers have rejected the idea that they must teach as they were taught, and have undoubtedly contributed hours and days of extra work to the task of being innovative teachers.

Most importantly, from our perspective as editors of this volume, it is evidently a **successful** process. It is made clear once again in these pages that teachers **do** make a difference, and for most students that difference marks the line between a lifetime of math avoidance or distaste, and a lifetime where mathematical skills and understanding are accessible.

We believe that teaching mathematics successfully requires exploring and thinking about how mathematics is learned. We believe that the chance to do such exploration is essential to mathematics teachers' professional growth. It certainly has been undertapped in the past, and understressed in all of the recent calls for an increased sense of professionalism among teachers. We are proud to be able to present this collection of accounts by teachers who **do** explore.

Mark Driscoll, Ph.D.
Jere Confrey, Ph.D.

December 1985

Mark Driscoll recently completed directing a two-year national Study of Exemplary Mathematics Programs for the Northeast Regional Exchange, Inc. (NEREX) in Chelmsford, Massachusetts. Currently Dr. Driscoll is directing a technical assistance project for urban mathematics collaboratives, funded by the Ford Foundation, and conducted by the Education Development Center in Newton, Massachusetts. He is the author of many articles and publications, including **Research Within Reach: Elementary School Mathematics** and **Research Within Reach: Secondary School Mathematics**—both distributed by the National Council of Teachers of Mathematics in Reston, Virginia. For further information on his work, contact:

Mark Driscoll, Ph.D.
Education Development Center, Inc.
55 Chapel Street
Newton, MA 02160

Jere Confrey currently teaches and does research in the area of mathematics education at Cornell University. She has been directly involved with schools and teachers in a variety of ways. For example, she was director of SummerMath at Mt. Holyoke College and she was a researcher/site visitor for the NEREX Study of Exemplary Mathematics Programs. Dr. Confrey is the author of many publications, including "What Should I Teach in Mathematics?" a chapter in **Educator's Handbook: A Research Perspective** (in press); "Mathematics Anxiety: A Person-Context-Adaptation Model," co-authored with Joan F. Mundy and Patricia Romney for the Annual Meeting of the American Educational Research Association, New Orleans, 1984; and "Concepts, Processes, and Mathematics Instruction" in **For the Learning of Mathematics,** July 1981. For further information on her work, contact:

Jere Confrey, Ph.D.
Department of Education
11 Stone Hall
Cornell University
Ithaca, NY 14853

MANIPULATIVE MATERIALS MAKE THE DIFFERENCE

by Joan McNichols

A fifth grade boy of above average ability has spent his school life in elementary classrooms in an affluent neighborhood. He was diagnosed as dyslexic at age seven by a licensed psychologist, and a "number disability" was noted in the report. The boy qualified for the resource specialists' program in his school and was admitted in the third-grade year.

Two years later, I met the boy after numerous attempts at the problem had been taken with tapes, records, flash cards, etc., and yet he still could not function with basic addition and subtraction facts, let alone the algorithms. Numbers were abstractions to him and even with the greatest efforts on his part and that of his family and teachers, he was not able to progress beyond the early first grade level in math.

I am introducing you to a dyscalculic. Dyscalculia, a specific number disability, has become less a mystery due to recent research. The remediation processes, however, are still scattered and involve much trial and error. Even though the most current research demonstrates that multisensory approaches are the most effective means of reaching the dyscalculic, many remediation programs are sadly lacking in manipulative materials.

Since the current emphasis in schools is on linear approaches to mastering competencies through behavioral objectives and computation drills, there is less time in the school programs for global, spatial, and logical experiences. This is where the dyscalculic child loses because he or she often has spatial and pictorial attributes that if tapped would make a positive mathematical experience available.

Some learning disabled children have difficulties in their input/output systems. Visual models are often practical tools to input information. If output is a difficulty, then the model makes a wonderful representational guide to use as a reference point from which to record.

Multisensory mathematics programs require the use of concrete materials (manipulatives) during the introduction of new concepts and as tools for understanding until a rationale is acquired. This issue has been addressed in the research listed in the bibliography of this article and was heavily emphasized by the National Council of Teachers of Mathematics in **Agenda For Action** for the 1980s where the use of concrete materials was closely associated with teaching mathematics more effectively during this decade.

Unfortunately for the remediator, mathematics is very diverse, consisting of many strands, many procedures, and many modalities (concrete, representational, and abstract). There is no panacea approach or magic "cure all." Therefore, all remediation should be preceded by appropriate diagnostics.

The area of diagnostics has been well researched and addressed by Dr. Patricia Davidson, author for the Cuisenaire Company of America, New Rochelle, New York. She has developed a Mathematics Diagnostic/Prescriptive Inventory (MDPI) for this purpose.

The four basic operations are often difficult for the dyscalculic. I relate this difficulty to the normal approach to teaching these operations, which is generally a very linear method depending on rote step-by-step memory procedures. Having accepted the potential nonlinear, spatial talents of the dyscalculic, I have applied a concrete approach with remarkable success using mainly multibase materials (base-10 blocks or Cuisenaire blocks, cubes, and rods).

I. Addition

Addition facts (upper decade):

The "Hungry Bug" addition (**Skateboard Addition and Subtraction,** Robertson, Laycock, and McLean) concentrates on creating "ten" or a "long" (decimeter stick) and counting out or adding on the residual.

The "Hungry Bug" activity can be introduced as a game with place value boards and base-10 materials where the goal of the Hungry Bug is always to become ten. Thus 9+6 is built with the base-10 materials as a train of nine units beside a train of six units:

The "nine-bug" always "eats" one unit to become a "ten-stick" plus five more or 1 long + 5 units or 15. This pattern of 9's can be carried on from 9+9 down to 9+1 as a game to reinforce the pattern. With older dyscalculics the pattern can be demonstrated without the game that is so appealing to young children.

This pattern is then transferred to the 8's where the "bug" eats two units, the 7's take three units, etc., down the scale to where the operations are more easily done in reverse. Example: 5+9 can be the 5-bug "eating" 5 plus 4 more or the 9-bug "eating" one plus 4 more for 14 in both cases.

The drill to follow the Hungry Bug activity can be done with dice games and base-10 materials that require trading or computer programmed activities that reinforce the concept.

Addition algorithm:

While the "Hungry Bug" is being practiced, addition problems of multiple digits can be done by using the base-10 materials and place value mats. The actual tactile and visual experience of making the trades plus the "talk" that goes on throughout the trades make the addition algorithm logical to the more spatial student. Many activities are available in **Skateboard Addition and Subtraction,** Activity Resources, Inc., Hayward, California.

II. Multiplication

The dyscalculic having difficulty with addition usually also has difficulty with multiplication. Multiplication facts through flash cards and rote approaches generally have been tried over and over again. No matter how big the prize offered, the learning disabled person does not succeed in learning them.

Skip-counting on a 100-chart is a good beginning for the 2's, 3's, 4's, and 5's to establish patterns in color. The visual pattern of a completed 100-chart of 2's shows ribbons of colors as all the even numbers are shaded. The 3-chart produces a diagonal pattern, etc.

Using colored cubes, the multiplication facts can be built into rectangular arrays and shaded on graph paper. This gives a wonderful visual representation of area as a unit of covering and gives a basic foundation for the understanding of prime numbers.

$2 \times 2 = 4$

$1 \times 4 = 4$
$4 \times 1 = 4$

While the array work is in process, a simple dice game, **Skyscrapers** (see **Enhance Chance,** Becker, Laycock and Waring, Activity Resources, Inc., Hayward, California), can be built from colored cubes as a model to extract the facts needed as the dice game progresses. The cube model is the most important aspect of this game, I believe, and must not be overlooked with the learning disabled child.

The 6's through 9's are cumbersome in array form and are most easily taught by using one's finger computer. The **fist** (clenched fist) represents 5 or half of base 10. Each raised finger is counted from five to the desired number. Example: 9×9 would be four fingers up on each hand with the fist having been five so four more fingers would be needed to get nine on each hand:

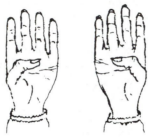

All fingers sticking up are counted as 10's or multiplied by 10 so we have 8 fingers up × 10 or 80 up. The fingers that are down (in this case the two thumbs) are multiplied (1×1=1) so 80+1=81.

This crutch has been magical to many dyscalculics and can be practiced almost anywhere since no materials are required except the fingers. I have witnessed learning disabled children become facile with their 6's through 9's in two lessons. Finally the digital computer is used for those facts that don't "stick" in the memory. The tactile unclogs the input system.

Multiplication Algorithm:

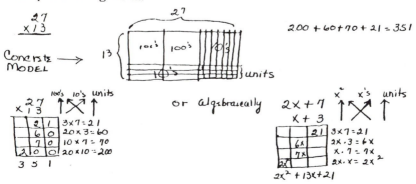

The rectangular array approach begun with the basic facts is key to understanding the multiplication algorithm and "seeing" the four partial products of two-digit times two-digit numbers that are so essential for basic algebra. The arrays at this level are built with base-10 materials rather than colored cubes.

Many activities to practice the rectangular array approach to multiplication can be found in **Skateboard Multiply and Divide,** McLean and Laycock, Activity Resources, Inc., Hayward, California.

III. Subtraction

Often the more spatial child finds subtraction and division easier than multiplication and addition because they are more spatially oriented skills.

"Hungry Bug" subtraction (subtraction facts—upper decade):

Instead of grouping to 10 as in the Hungry Bug addition, the process is reversed and all numbers are taken out of ten or compared to ten when subtracting, with the residual added on. Example: $18-9$ would be seen with base-10 materials as the difference between 10 and 9 or **one plus eight** = 9, whereas $15-6$ would be seen as $10-6$ or the difference between 10 and 6 or $4+5=9$. This pattern of always subtracting or comparing with ten is a picture easily visualized by a spatial child if experienced with base-10 materials and can be applied to the subtraction algorithm immediately.

Subtraction algorithm:

Subtraction with the base-10 materials should be introduced as comparison as well as "take-away." Example: $32-18=14$

Comparison: Build 32 out of base-10 materials
Cover with 18 built of base-10 materials
What amount is not covered?

From the base-10 model, this can first be represented on centimeter paper and cut out with scissors.

Take Away: Build 32 on a place value board with base-10 materials
Trade one of the tens for ten units before taking 18 away
This can be represented as:

$$\begin{array}{r} \overset{2}{\overset{}{\cancel{3}}}\,\overset{12}{\cancel{2}} \\ -\,1\ 8 \\ \hline 14 \end{array}$$

As long as base-10 materials and place value boards are used, no amount of zeros in the minuend will be confusing.

To the learning disabled child, the comparison method presents a spatial model that often makes more sense than the take-away model.

IV. Division

Division is a very spatial concept and children can grasp it quickly if it is approached with appropriate concrete models and late enough in the children's neurological development. The rote sequence of DMSB (Divide, Multiply, Subtract, Bring down), however, is very confusing to children and makes little sense.

"Divvy up" division is the most common approach to division by young children but not necessarily the most reasonable to the spatial child. In "divvy-up" division, $2)\overline{6}$ or $6 \div 2$, the child takes six units or counters and continues to pass them out back and forth between two people until all possible are gone with both people having an even amount. In this case each person gets three. In $7 \div 2$, the same routine is used but there will be one left or the child will have to split the remaining one in half.

The "measure-out" method of division is often better visualized by the spatial child and is a tremendous foundation for division of fractions. In $6 \div 2$, the student measures out the six counters in groups of two until he has three groups.

Division Algorithm:

Division problems with large or small dividends, with or without remainders, can be introduced with single-digit divisors at the same time if a solid foundation of array work has been accomplished before introducing the algorithm.

Example: 294÷3 would be built with base-10 materials as 2 flats (100's), 9 longs (tens), and 4 units:

The student is asked the questions as follows:

1. Can you give each of your 3 guests a flat?
   No (Trade the flats for 20 longs)

2. Can you give each guest a long?
   Yes

3. How many? (Either the "divvy-up" or "measure-out" method is used to determine 9 groups or 9 longs for each person with two left over.) The 9 is recorded in the 10's place in the problem and the 27 given away are subtracted from the 29 to leave 2 longs to be traded for units. The problem at this point looks like this:

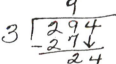

The two longs and 4 units have now become 24 units.

4. How many units can you give each person? Using "divvy-up" or "measure-out" methods, the answer of 8 is obtained and recorded as below:

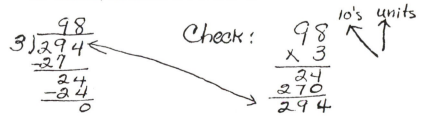

Practice with arrays plus games emphasizing concepts of multiplication and division with the rectangular array as a base are included in **Skateboard Multiply and Divide,** McLean and Laycock, Activity Resources, Hayward, California.

Interactive computer programs using base-10 materials have been published by Cuisenaire Company of America, New Rochelle, New York, and make good, meaningful drill and practice that is spatially oriented for all four operations. They also include good estimation practice that is often a natural approach for a visual/spatial learner.

Conclusion

I have described the core of the basic structured multisensory program used with the dyscalculic boy presented in the introduction of this chapter. He and I began working in September of his fifth grade year. By the time the standardized tests were given in his elementary school in the spring, he was testing at the fourth grade level in math. In addition to feeling more confident about himself, he had begun to enjoy math. We met twice a week for an hour and his resource teacher followed through with many of the same techniques in his daily sessions at the school. He was always pleased to hear that she was working closely with me and that he would be doing the same kind of math at school as he did in his private sessions. If a "make-up lesson" were required, he had no trouble concentrating for a two-hour session from time to time and would often respond with, "Is the long session over already?"

This article has been aimed at the dyscalculic child, and the activities as well as the resources cited are particularly successful in remediating dyscalculic children. Their usefulness, however, extends to all children whose learning style leans toward the visual/spatial. Preparatory diagnostics with these children are important for finding the appropriate modalities to include in the prescribed instruction. The clinical interview approach to diagnostics covered beautifully by Ed Labinowicz in **Learning From Children,** Addison-Wesley, 1985, has been the most productive for me with the dyscalculic. This approach allows the diagnostician a chance to interact with the student and observe behaviors and responses far beyond that possible on any written test. These observations and responses are important guidelines for subsequent prescriptions. For me, the combination of clinical interviews and prescribed visual/spatial activities has proved highly successful with dyscalculic children. Many teachers and many children can benefit from their use as an alternative to more traditional approaches to teaching mathematical concepts and skills.

Joan McNichols is the Mathematics Specialist at the Newport Center for Educational Therapy in Newport Beach, California. For further information on her program for the dyscalculic, contact:

Joan McNichols
Mathematics Specialist
Newport Center for Educational Therapy
2854 Alta Vista Drive
Newport Beach, CA 92660

REFERENCES

Joffee, L. 1980. "School Mathematics and Dyslexia: Aspects of the Interrelationship" (Ph.D. Thesis, University of Aston, Birmingham, U.K.)

Labinowicz, E. 1985. **Learning From Children,** Addison-Wesley, Menlo Park, CA.

Laycock, M. 1974. **Base Ten Math,** Activity Resources, Inc., Hayward, CA.

Laycock, M. and G. Watson. 1971. **The Fabric of Mathematics,** Activity Resources, Inc., Hayward, CA.

"Math Genius May Have Hormonal Basis." **Science,** December 1983, vol. 222, no. 4630.

Davidson, P. "Mathematics Diagnostic-Prescriptive Inventory." Unpublished manuscript.

"An Agenda For Action." 1980. National Council of Teachers of Mathematics, Reston, VA.

Sawyer, W. 1943. **Mathematician's Delight,** Penguin, Baltimore, MD.

YANKEE INGENUITY: A MATH PROGRAM BUILT FROM NECESSITY

by Sandra F. Murphy

It is the intention of this article to describe and analyze a math curriculum program I designed to use in a second grade classroom. I will discuss the reasons for its organization, its application in the classroom, and the reasons I believe it works.

This project developed out of necessity. It grew from the need to recognize and accept the span of math abilities and understandings in a typical classroom. It grew from a need to meet the individual requirements of students.

Upon entering the public school system, I was given a curriculum guide for math and a standard math workbook, one for each child. My first year of teaching I tried to use the math workbook with all of my students. By October it was evident my students' math skills were as varied as all their other abilities. I tried to supplement the math workbook with various games, manipulatives, and additional work for more advanced students. In the teachers' room, I discovered some outdated workbooks and let my advanced math students work in them as well as their regular text. My enthusiasm about how well they did seemed to breed in them a desire to do more math. I hated to see children waiting for other children so I said, "You can all just go ahead and work at your own pace." It was something I knew I had to say. I hated holding children back, but what a mistake it was! The eager students did reams of math, producing piles of correcting work for me. The gap between my students grew wider. But the biggest problem of all was the sequence of pages in the math workbook. It was built on the idea that a teacher introduces a "new concept" and then there are a few pages for the child to work on. Then another new concept, and a few more pages. Quite often these concepts are unrelated. Quite often what the teacher is teaching is how to do the workbook page, not a new understanding. Because of this I was constantly in demand. I felt that I'd never catch up, and there were times I wanted to cancel math altogether because of the number of questions being fired at me. I knew students didn't learn math from a workbook. I made games and activities using hands-on materials, yet there seemed to be no organized way to use them. The games were used as a reward—when children were finished their assigned work, they could go play with the math games. It seemed that the good math students played many games while the children who would most benefit from playing the games had difficulty completing the assigned work with extra time for game playing. I decided I needed to incorporate the math games into the assigned work.

It was clear to me that there had to be a better way to teach math. Teaching to the whole group didn't make sense. I don't teach reading to a class of twenty-four; so why is it acceptable to teach math to the whole class? Yet allowing children to work independently in such a hodgepodge fashion had a quick burnout rate for the teacher.

I survived the first year but knew I couldn't begin with a new class and teach math in the same format. I analyzed the second grade math curriculum, listed the range of abilities my students possessed when entering second grade, and sequenced the order in which I felt students conceptualized math at this level. I concluded that much of the workbook was considered "exposure to"; yet I feel it doesn't make sense to "expose" children to place value, or regroup for addition and subtraction, for example, when they have not internalized simple addition. My goal was for my students to work at their own pace, at their own level—and for what they could do, to be able to do it well. I felt it was better to go on to third grade being good at addition and subtraction, rather than being exposed to the entire second grade curriculum and not being good at any of it.

I gave a great deal of thought on how to develop a math program that would work and on what was important to incorporate in curriculum design. These are my conclusions:

1. **Ownership of the work.** It is important for a child to have a sense that it is his or her math work, that it is appropriate, and that he or she can choose what to work on and when. In this sense, math belongs to each individual student.

2. **Short-term goals.** By having realistic short-term goals, children can reach their goals and feel a sense of accomplishment. This allows each child to feel successful and gives a child confidence in doing math.

3. **Varied experiences in math.** Adults as well as children get bored by a lack of variety. Variety is the spice of life and crucial in curriculum design.

4. **Consistent format.** To help this program work, it is important from the beginning to establish consistency. Children follow directions very quickly if things are well explained and then remain in the same format. For an individualized program to work well, it is important for children to become aware of how to work on their own. This frees the teacher to teach and assist those children who need help. It also encourages children to think on their own and make decisions.

5. **Peer interaction.** This program encourages peers to interact. Math games are incorporated into the program at every level. Children become the teachers of games. They are expected to teach children how to play the games and to check games children have done individually. Children assist in explaining how to do workbook pages; it is encouraging to hear one child explain to another how to do a graph or how to bundle groups of ten, for example.

6. **Review.** Constant review is an important component of the math program. At each level there is a review of what was learned in the previous levels.

From these six givens in curriculum design, I developed a math program to suit my needs. The math program has five components. It is color-coded and carefully sequenced. (A list of color codes and sample cover sheet appear at the end of this chapter.)

1. Each colored folder has a standard cover sheet which describes the components. The cover sheet is the key to the entire folder; it details the work to be done. As each piece of work is done, it is checked off on the cover sheet.

2. The math workbook, which is required in the public school system I teach in, became a part of the program by my selecting appropriate pages for each of the math concepts I planned to teach. Each folder cover sheet lists specific workbook pages for the student to complete. For example, the yellow folder may list pages 23, 25, 27, 77, and 79. Many of the workbook pages are not used because I feel they are not worth the time it would take to explain how to do the page. Students keep their own workbooks in their desks and rip out the appropriate pages for each folder.

3. The third component comprises related worksheets, each sequenced, color-coded, and self-explanatory. All worksheets are set up in an accessible file so that the students can collect their own worksheets and other materials.

4. The fourth component comprises math games. These games are clearly labeled and boxed according to color. For example, RED GAME 1, RED GAME 2.

5. The fifth component is called "counting cans." Each folder has four cans; each contains a specific number of items to be counted. RED CAN #1 may have 21 plastic dogs. RED CAN #2 may have 30 yellow wooden triangles. The child counts the items and records his/her answer on the cover sheet. Money folders have money to count; counting by 5's folder has nickels to count; place value has sticks to bundle.

When I introduce the math program to the class, I introduce a component each day. I explain how the work is to be done and checked off on the cover sheet. The first folder is very simple because I am mainly interested in teaching the procedure. After all the components are introduced, we are on our way and soon everyone is working at his or her own level.

This may sound very complicated, and putting it all together does take a great deal of time; however, the time is well spent. My students always love math and they are disappointed in me if a day goes by and we don't have math. I have had some students doing solid third grade math and other students still mastering addition and subtraction, but no one seemed to feel any sense of failure. It is clear everyone is doing what is right for him or her. Everyone seems pleased when a peer moves on to a new folder.

I give the children daily feedback on the covers of their folders. The child receives comments about his/her work completed the day before. This provides an accurate record of each child's progress.

There is a bit of protocol that the children consider important. When a child finishes a folder, he or she brings it to the teacher, who adds positive reviews to the front of the folder. Next, the child selects the appropriate color for his or her next folder, color-codes the cover sheet and staples it inside the folder, and then is ready to go to work. The entire folder of completed work is taken home.

Parents are informed of the math program. On Parents' Night, they work in their child's math folder and get a first-hand sense of what is involved. Parents then appreciate a completed math folder when it comes home. These folder rituals seem like simple aspects of the math program, yet they help the program succeed.

But when do you teach??? This answer has two parts:

The children who usually are the first to begin a new concept are those students who are good at math. It is usually quite simple to work with them individually in small groups and introduce new concepts. These students can then be used to assist in working with other students. I have found they are most helpful in explaining how to do something rather than actually teaching a concept.

The second part of this answer is that much of the math curriculum at this level is simply practice—getting good with numbers. If the concepts are sequenced appropriately, and the children have ample activities with numbers, the math concepts are not difficult to teach. Usually the teacher is working with very small groups and is able to detect where a child is having difficulty. Along with the math folders, I always have some part of the day when we do whole group math activities. These usually are incorporated into the morning exercise time. We have three exercise leaders for each day. They lead the class in an exercise and decide what we will say while we do their exercise. For example, a leader might say, "jumping jacks and counting by 5's to 100." Another leader might say, "jogging in place and counting by 2's to 50." The children become quite interested in inventing new exercises—"helicopters," "whirlybirds," "crab walk." The rote part of the exercises varies and includes, for example, saying the months or the days of the week.

One student, Jeff, I remember in particular. He benefited tremendously from the math program. Jeff entered second grade far behind in reading, with a poor self-concept, and a severe speech problem. Jeff had an innate math ability and he was a hard worker. He became very excited about his ability to do math, and he was pleased he could work at his own pace. He was soon way ahead of his peers. He was extremely proud of himself, and this success seemed to help him in other areas. He was still behind in reading, and his speech greatly affected his spelling; yet his success with math allowed him to respect himself and me as his teacher. The math program gave Jeff the chance to be good at something and feel successful. Years later I ran into Jeff. He was in the sixth grade, and I asked him how school was going. The first thing he said, with a big grin, was, "I've got a 99% average in math!" I think the smile on my face was as big as his.

In conclusion, some elements seem essential to the foundation of the curriculum design I have described. It is essential the students have short-term goals and a sense of ownership. It is essential the program be consistent in its format, but the work be varied and exciting. Peer interaction should be encouraged and review built into its design. Mathematics should occur all day long in many different ways. A good teacher never misses an opportunity to teach math.

HOW TO GET STARTED WITH YOUR OWN MATH PROGRAM

1. List the important concepts you want to cover in your grade level. Your curriculum guide and math book can help. Don't forget to review some concepts from the preceding grade and also include some more difficult concepts for enrichment.

2. Sequence these concepts.

3. Look around your classroom and school for resources to incorporate (games, cards, math kits, ditto masters, etc.)

4. Write your cover sheets for each folder using some workbook or math book pages, worksheets, games, counting cans, or whatever you have available. Try to incorporate activities and look for worksheets that are interesting but have simple directions.

5. Assign a color to each folder and mark that color clearly on the top of the worksheets, games, etc.

6. Set up a color-coded file of worksheets so that children can get their own. Keep materials easily accessible and clearly marked.

7. Collect or create some games and box them according to colors. If a game doesn't fit in the game box, put in a card describing the game and its location. If you do not have enough games, use card games (such as "21," "war," "99," "five in a row"), bean bag tosses, "Little Professors," etc.

8. Make counting cans by collecting interesting objects and containers. My multiplication cans have red pegs that are worth 3, blue pegs valued at 4, and other colors with different values. The children have to multiply by the value of the pegs and add up the totals. The easier cans may have 37 pine cones or 52 bottle caps.

SECOND GRADE MATH FOLDERS

1.	pink	first grade review (addition, subtraction, number order, counting shapes, etc.)
2.	tan	addition I (sums to 20)
3.	dark green	subtraction I (minuends to 20)
4.	brown	sequencing and ordering numbers to 100, counting by 1's, 2's, 5's, and 10's to 100
5.	red	mixed addition and subtraction (1 and 2 digit addition and subtraction without regrouping, column addition)
6.	yellow	place values (1's, 10's, and 100's)
7.	dark blue	money (coin recognition and counting)
8.	white	addition II (addition with regrouping)
9.	black	word problems (addition and subtraction)
10.	light green	multiplication (a conceptual introduction)
11.	light blue	telling time (to nearest 5 minutes)
12.	orange	subtraction II (with regrouping)
13.	gray	fractions
14.	purple	mixed addition and subtraction with regrouping
15.	rainbow	equations (missing addends and subtrahends, etc.)

EXAMPLE COVER SHEET STAPLED INTO A TAN FOLDER

(1) (2)

Tan
+
Addition 1
with some subtraction

Name :
Date Begun :
Date Finished :

Worksheets
(child colors in when completed) (Teacher stars if worksheet has been corrected + is perfect)

Tan	1	↓	✓
Tan	2	▓	✗
Tan	3	▓	✗
Tan	4	▓	
Tan	5		
Tan	6		
Tan	7		
Tan	8		
Tan	9		
Tan	10		

Consumable Math Book Pages
FRONT   BACK

Page 27 + 28	▓	✗
Page 29 + 30		
Page 31 + 32		
Page 181 + 182		
Page 183 + 184		
Page 73 + 74		
Page 105 + 106		
Page 107 + 108		
Page 109 + 110		
Page 111 + 112		

Counting Cans
child puts number here   Teacher stars if correct

Tan 1	↓	↓
Tan 2	**76**	✗
Tan 3		

Games
child colors when completed   Teacher stars if checked

Tan	1	▓	✗
Tan	2		
Tan	3		
Tan	4		

Some whole-group class activities:

> fractions, measurement, telling time, counting, flash cards to learn the addition and subtraction facts, graphing, word problems.

Brown

Numbers

1 2 3 4

Name:

Date Begun:

Date Finished:

Worksheets

brown 1		
brown 2		
brown 3		
brown 4		
brown 5		
brown 6		
brown 7		
brown 8		
brown 9		
brown 10		

Math Book Pages

page 45+46		
page 11+12		
page 13+14		
page 35+36		
page 37+38		
page 39+40		
page 49+50		
page 164		
page 165+166		
page 167+168		

Counting Cans

brown 1		
brown 2		
brown 3		

Games

brown 1		
brown 2		
brown 3		
brown 4		

Sandra F. Murphy is a first grade teacher at the Garden Street School in Milford, New Hampshire. She moves with her first graders on to second grade; the curriculum described in this article is adapted for the first graders. For further information, contact:

Sandra F. Murphy
9 Union Street
Milford, NH 03055

IN SEARCH OF THE WOOZLE

by Bernadine Krawczyk

Introduction

Pooh stopped and bent over studying the tracks in a puzzled sort of way. Piglet didn't have anything to do until Friday, so he didn't mind going with Pooh "in case they turned out to be Hostile Animals"; or possibly, it really was a Woozle! Winnie the Pooh looked at the tracks again, "You mean in case it really is two Woozles." So off they went together, pursuing something. As it turned out, Pooh and Piglet had walked in a circle and were really following their own tracks.

Searching for the Woozle is an adventure in problem solving. The circle is our template or theme for the adventure but any other concept could as easily be used. Since problem solving is an exercise in imagination, we watch Pooh study his own tracks, create a big unknown, and undaunted, press on. So it is when children solve problems.

From their earliest years children attempt to answer questions about themselves and their own world. They are little investigators observing, collecting data, and drawing conclusions. Mathematical activities can develop these abilities through sorting, graphing, estimating, measuring, and patterning. As they begin to recognize, classify, and compare, they also question and verbalize. They want to keep records of their findings, first through pictures, and eventually they learn abstract representations. Throughout this process it is important to maximize the child's active involvement.

Meaningful experiences with concrete objects quickly teach a child to be flexible when applying a new set of ideas to a problem. Thus, Piglet thought it was one set of tracks and Pooh thought it was two. How beautiful it is to discover that in problem solving there can be more than one solution.

Making a Circle

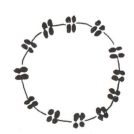

But what do we know about a circle? As mathematicians we know that a circle is a powerful concept in that two definitions of it create the same object. Those are equal distance from a point and constant curvature. A child's understanding of a circle involves such attributes as roundness, circular, without corners. They may see a circle in ovals, ellipses, eights or other closed curves. Through multiple activities it is our goal to help children come closer to an understanding of what is meant by a circle.

It is important when introducing a concept to a young child to involve the child's whole body in the activity. An activity as simple as standing in the circle enables the child, through gross motor involvement, to begin sensing roundness. The child can see the physical circle made by classmates, can sense the curving in either direction from his or her point on the circle, and can hear the word. Another way you can personalize the circle concept, while also establishing visual and spatial awareness, is to have the children again form a circle. This time pair them and ask them to trace each other's footprints on a piece of paper. Then have them step back two or three steps to see the circle they have made. You could also use contact paper. Cut out the footprints and stick them to the floor to establish a permanent place for each child to stand when making a circle. You will note that both ideas use several modalities of learning and emphasize the concrete approach to making circles.

Circle Search

Searching for circles in our environment is one of the best ways to develop visual awareness and visual thinking. Optimize rather than minimize circle experiences. Go searching for "roundness" in the classroom or outside on the playground. Ask the children to look at home, perhaps in the kitchen or another room in the house, or even in the grocery store. The search is endless and the list inexhaustable. Don't forget that younger children may need limitations such as "Find ten round things." The enjoyable part of this assignment is that no two people will find the same ten things, and the children will begin seeing things they might otherwise have missed.

The outdoor environment offers unlimited possibilities for discovering round things. Nature honors diversity. Nothing is lovelier than looking at a flower and discovering what is "round" about the flower. And in that flower a child will also discover a sense of number as well as symmetry.

When you are outdoors, the children can be divided into teams of two (three is the proverbial "crowd") to look for "round" things. They can record their findings either in picture form or with a list of words. A sturdy piece of cardboard with paper stapled to the top makes a good writing or drawing surface. Remember to give them both a time limit and an area limit, i.e., no farther than the school fence. This activity also encourages the development of language arts skills and vocabulary.

While the children are gathering information they also can be "squirrels." Give each team self-closing plastic bags so they can gather round things such as small pebbles, acorns, sticks, leaves, bottle caps, aluminum can tabs. Remind them not to pull up plants or destroy the environment. Once the "squirrels" have completed their assignment and it is time to return to the classroom, have them bring all their treasures back. It is now time to discuss their findings and the contents of their "squirrel" bags which will be added to your collection of things in squirrel boxes.

Sorting

Mary Baratta-Lorton in her program, "Mathematics Their Way," calls her sorting boxes "junk" boxes. It is questionable today, with the use of so many manipulatives in the classroom, whether teachers really do have "junk"; is it really "good garbage" or just a collection? Whatever you call it (I prefer to use the term squirrel boxes), you want your students to consider it a mathematics tool similar to textbooks, pattern blocks, or a ruler.

A good way to start squirrel boxes at the beginning of the school year is to tell the class that the items in the boxes were stored there by the squirrels who are saving them for winter. You can invite the class to add the contents of their squirrel bags to the collection. This establishes their ownership in the project. However, they must understand, once they empty those bags, the items belong to the squirrels; they can't go home in pockets or book bags.

The squirrel boxes can be any size; just do not use boxes that are too big. Cigar box size is good or even smaller boxes. They do not all have to be the same size. The boxes can be filled with many things, usually only one type of item in a box, but this is not a fixed rule never to be broken. Good "round" or curved objects include paper clips, buttons, dried macaroni or pasta, lima beans, nuts and bolts, screws, plastic bread fasteners or any other small items, in addition to the contents of the squirrel bags.

First, ask the students to shake the box; pose the question, "What do you think is inside?" As the students begin to use all their senses to make decisions about the contents, ask thought-provoking questions like, "Is it hard or soft; big or small; metal or wood?" "Is the box heavy or light?" "What shape is it?" "How do you know?" The students also begin to develop a sense of volume by guessing whether the box is full, half full or has only a little bit inside. After these preliminary activities, let the students open the boxes to see what is inside.

Discuss the reasons for their guesses. This is a good time to develop deductive reasoning skills by explaining how people reach one answer and eliminate another possibility—e.g., it rolled so I knew it wasn't something flat.

Next have each student take a handful of contents from the squirrel box and replace the lid. Estimate how many objects are in the handful. Estimate how many more are in the box. Count, if it's important to know an exact answer; otherwise you can proceed with sorting activities.

Sorting is looking for critical attributes. An attribute is a characteristic describing one particular property which some objects have in common. Younger or less experienced students may not know what sorting means. Ask them to divide the handful of objects from their squirrel box into two piles. This very open-ended activity encourages divergent thinking and allows for more than one correct answer. Be sure to go around and ask each student what attribute was used to sort the handful. Encourage the students to think analytically and to express their thoughts. After this initial exercise, ask them to focus on one property or attribute and to sort the handful again.

The students should continue this activity using more of the contents of their squirrel box. Sorting attributes can include categories such as size, shape, color, texture, design, and use. Encourage the formation of three, four, or even five sets. Younger or less experienced students may have difficulty maintaining consistent sorting criteria as they continue forming sets. Keep encouraging them and praise their successful efforts. The mental processing helps students discover similarities as well as differences and is a prerequisite for the higher-level skills of set inclusion, intersection, and null sets. The sorting activities can also be displayed and recorded as a graph.

Graphing

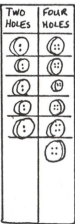

Graphs are an excellent way to summarize completed sorting and squirrel box activities. Students can organize and record the information in graph form, giving them a chance to see relationships, discover patterns, analyze the information and develop number sense.

Beginning graph experiences are often "real graphs." Students use real objects, such as buttons, that have been sorted into at least two categories, and physically line them up on a flat surface covered with white butcher paper. This physical representation allows the students to see the one-to-one correspondence of sorted objects to the categories used for sorting. If the paper is ruled off, this one-to-one correspondence will be even clearer. Give the various categories used to sort objects a label that corresponds to the classification.

The next step is to analyze the data. Good questions will reveal a great deal of information that might otherwise be overlooked, and you will learn a great deal about the thinking and mental processing that took place. This is another opportunity to develop and expand mathematical vocabulary by using terms such as "greater than," "fewer than," "more than," "less than," and "how many."

Graphs can help students do many things: help organize data, see relationships, discover patterns, compare information, and make personal choices. Make an informal personal opinion graph by drawing a circle on the board and dividing it in half. Pose a question and put tally marks in the proper half to indicate answers. Use questions such as: Do you think it will rain today? Did you do your homework? Did you remember your library book? Hot lunch today?

These are yes/no questions but others can and will be open-ended, while some will have exact answers. The possibilities are endless for questions that develop thinking skills, environmental awareness, and counting skills while keeping with the "roundness" theme.

- How many buttons are you wearing? Think; estimate; then count.
- How many zeros in all the numerals 1 to 100?
- Name round fruits and vegetables (younger children can draw pictures).
- What color are your eyes?

Estimation

Estimation skills are necessary for everyday living and they lead to more sophisticated skills such as measurement, computing percentage, and rounding off. For example, without estimation skills it would be difficult cooking for six people; they would either leave the table hungry or need a walk-in refrigerator to hold the leftovers.

Having an estimating jar in your classroom is a good learning experience for your students. The jar can be any size; however, with younger or less experienced students, use a small jar—the same for each estimation activity—and fill it to the top. This establishes continuity and the size is manageable for them. The jar should be easy to fill and count. In keeping with the Woozle theme, some possible round or curved items you might use are walnuts, jelly beans, peanuts, grapes, pennies, buttons, acorns, pine cones, or paper clips. Change the contents often because the more they do it, the better your students will be at making predictions and checking those predictions, and connecting abstract ideas to real world concepts. Estimation jars are good for anytime—before school work, transition "sponge" time between classes or subjects, or even as a class or school contest.

When there is an estimation jar in the classroom, students are as curious as raccoons. Their questions are endless: What is it? Why is it here? How come? The teacher needs to nurture this curiosity through meaningful questions:
- How many in the jar?
- More or less than in the last jar?
- How many in a handful? Two handfuls.
- More than 10? Less than 100?

As students estimate, write their answers on the board. Finding the exact number in the jar is not always necessary. If you want to know if the jar has more than 10, count out that amount and draw some conclusions. The same can be done for 100. A more experienced group can extend the estimation activities by counting the objects into groups of ten. This makes the task easier and also adds place value to the counting part of the lesson.

Measurement

Sorting, graphing and estimation are concepts that deal with making comparisons. Measurement also deals with comparisons. But to learn the concept of measurement, you need to measure something. Because younger children do not understand what a tape measure, ruler, or yardstick does, use a piece of string to measure things.

Young children enjoy measuring and comparing. A natural place to start is with the round parts of the body such as fingers, head, arm, leg, trunk. Ask how big and how long as a way of encouraging a measurement set of activities which can be done with two students working together. Use a piece of string to measure length of an arm and cut the string off at the exact length of the arm. Repeat the measuring and cutting for other parts of the body. Record or graph the pieces of string by taping them down sequentially from the longest to the shortest and labeling them.

To carry this lesson one step further, try body measurement using a stuffed animal such as a teddy bear. The children will enjoy this novel idea and begin making comparisons to find differences and similarities between themselves and others. And Winnie the Pooh would just love to have his belly measured.

Circle Puzzles and Tessellations

Remember the old adage, looks can be deceiving? Well, so far we have explored the uses of the circle in a wide variety of experiential activities that are challenging as well as fun. The next activities explore the unusual things circles can do when they are taken apart.

Use a coffee lid as a pattern to trace a circle on construction paper. Cut the circle out and cut it into three to six parts, as such:

It is a good idea to store the pieces in self-closing bags so the puzzles can be exchanged with neighbors for an additional challenge or put on a table as an activity station.

Now try the following with a piece of construction paper. Again use the coffee can lid to draw a circle and then cut it out. Put it aside. Draw the lines as suggested and cut along the lines. This puzzle is somewhat more challenging since you are working in negative space.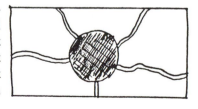

Explaining to the students that they are actually building around the empty circular shape makes the negative concept easier for them to understand, and gives them a hint on how to put the puzzle together.

To form a mosaic pattern or tessellation, use two pieces of different colored construction paper. Trace several circles on each piece of paper and cut them out.

Each circular piece is then folded in fourths and cut on the fold to make fractional circle pieces. Then the challenge of a very sophisticated kind of visualization begins. It is a good idea to make several sample cards ahead of time but even asking the students to duplicate these can prove difficult. For some reason, those little pieces you have on your sample just do not look like the pieces the student has. It takes time and experimentation for the student to realize the task really is not very difficult and is a whole lot of fun. Once they get the idea, they will be ready to make their own pattern designs. The following are only a few suggestions; there are more ideas like these for older grade levels in **Arithmetic Teacher,** January 1978.

As a final thought, you might want your students to assemble this entire set of activities into a booklet. Several pages can be devoted to each activity and a nice wallpaper cover (with circle designs) adds a finishing touch. It is a good take-home item for students to share with parents, and it also gives parents a chance to see what is going on in math class.

The list of activities related to the circle can be as endless as the circle itself. Other themes, similar to this, can be developed for other geometric shapes or even for colors or for themes such as "Teddy Bear Day" or "Math Week." Use your creativity, your thinking skills, and search for your own Woozle.

Bernie Krawczyk is a second grade teacher in Stratford, Connecticut. She has conducted numerous workshops throughout the State. "In Search of the Woozle" was recently presented as a K-3 workshop at the 1985 A.T.O.M.I.C. Conference in Willimantic, Connecticut. For further information on her program, contact:

Bernadine Krawczyk
1841 Huntington Turnpike
Trumbull, CT 06611

REFERENCES

Baratta-Lorton, Mary. 1976. **Mathematics Their Way.** Menlo Park, CA: Addison-Wesley.

Burns, Marilyn. **The Math Solution.** Sausalito, CA: Marilyn Burns Education Associates.

Dana, Marcia. 1978. "The Surprising Circle." **Arithmetic Teacher:** Vol. 25, No. 4, 4-10.

van Delft, Pieter and Jack Botermans. 1978. **Creative Puzzles of the World.** New York; Harry N. Abrams, Inc.

Vitale, Barbara Meister. 1982. **Unicorns Are Real.** Rolling Hills Estates, California: Jalmar Press.

FRACTION GAMES—
VISIONS AND REVISIONS

by Albert B. Bennett, Jr. and Peter Schiot

> Time for you and time for me,
> And time yet for a hundred indecisions,
> And for a hundred visions and revisions,
> Before the taking of a toast and tea.
>
> from The Love Song of J. Alfred Prufrock
> by T.S. Eliot

Playing games has long been recognized as a method of teaching mathematical concepts and skills to obtain student involvement and enthusiasm. However, the potential for motivation and learning when students revise games or create their own games is not as well known. In the article, "Mathematics Students Have a Right to Write," from the May 1983 issue of **The Arithmetic Teacher,** Joan Shaw notes that devising games requires the three essential elements of writing: prewriting (inventing and creating); writing (stating rules); and rewriting (trying the game and making adjustments). The purpose of the following article is to describe the activities of a fifth grade class which was exposed to the combination of reading-writing process and mathematical games.

As part of their instruction in the reading-writing process, the students learned to assume responsibility and control of their own learning by continually questioning and evaluating everything they read and write. They were encouraged to develop critical judgement and made to feel their ideas and views were worthwhile. In their mathematics instruction the students were taught published games for learning about fractions.[1]

An unexpected outcome was the spontaneous desire of many of the students to revise the given games or to create their own games. By revising published games, and in most cases producing more sophisticated games, the students had a means of measuring their accomplishments. The student became the author and inventor, teaching his or her own rules to other students and adults. As owner of the game, the student became responsible for its improvement, playing and revising the game many times while sharing and exchanging strategies and knowledge of fractions. At the beginning of the school year each student was issued a deck of fraction bars. These bars represent halves, thirds, fourths, sixths, and twelfths. The bars can be described before fractions are introduced by stating the total number of parts and the number of shaded parts. For example, one of the bars shown here has 12 parts and 5 parts are shaded; or, 5 out of 12 parts are shaded. Counting the zero-bars (no parts shaded) up to the whole-bars (all parts shaded) there are 32 different bars.

The teacher introduced the fraction games by showing each game to one or two students. The students were then responsible for teaching the game to their classmates. A grid with the names of the students and games showed who was responsible for each game and which students had played the game. As examples, Emily (EW) was responsible for teaching **Double or Nothing** as she taught this game to 23 students; and Dan and Amy were responsible for teaching Fraction Bingo.

	Match	Five Bars	Small Step Race	Double or Nothing	FRIO	Flip	Adding Game	Capture	Difference Race	Spin and Race	Exact Fits	Concentration	Black Jack	Diffe	Fraction Rummy	Hi Lo Race	Bars and Cards	Roll and Race	Fraction Bingo
Abby	HB	T	J.W.	EW	AB	AR	S.h	JS	HW	A(	AB	HC	?	MK	D.W.	KH	CS	J.O	Amy
Alex	HB	AB	J.W.	EW	AB	T	S.h	JS	HW	A(	AO	HC	?	MK	J.W.	KH	CS	J.O	Dan
Alie	HB	AB	J.W.	EW	AB	AR	S.h	JS	HW	Al	Ao	HC	?	HK	D.W.	KH	CS	J.O	Amy Dan
llison	HB	AB	J.W.	EW	AB	AR	S.h	JS	HW	AC	AS	HC	?	MK	D.W.	KH	CS	J.O	Dan
Amy	HB	AB	J.W.	EW	A.B	AR	S.h	JS	HW	AC	BJ	HC	?	MK	J.W.	KH	CS	J.O	Dan
Bill	HB	AB	J.W.	EW	A.B	AR	S.h	JS	HW	AC	BJ	HC	?	MK	J.W.	KH	CS	J.O	Amy
Chikayo	HB	AB	J.W.	EW	AB	AR	S.h	JS	HW	A(	AB	HC	?	MK	J.W.	KH	CS	J.O	Dan
Danny	HB	AB	J.W.	EW	AB	AR	S.h	JS	HW	BC	RJ	HC	?	MK	D.W.	KH	CS	J.O	Dan
Emily	HB	AB	J.W.	T	AB	AR	S.h	JS	HW	AC	AO	HC	Dan	MK	D.W.	KH	CS	J.O	Amy
Heath...									HW	Al	AJ	HC				H	CS	J.O	

In addition to spending time on computation and problem solving during the first two months, the students played games with fraction bars. During this time they did not use fraction numerals or terminology. As examples, a ¾ bar was described as "three parts out of four" and ⅙ as "one part out of six."

After the games had been played a few times some students began to change the rules to improve the games or make them more challenging. Here is one of the games which was taught by the teacher. This game provides readiness for addition.

FRACTION BAR BLACK JACK   *(addition)*

<u>Players</u>   2-4

<u>Materials</u>   Fraction bars

Spread the bars face down.

The object is to use 1 or more bars to get a total shaded amount which is equal to <u>1 whole bar</u> or as close to <u>1 whole bar</u> as possible without going "over".

Each player takes 1 bar at a time. After taking all the bars he/she wants, the player says, "I'm holding".

After every player has said, "I'm holding", the players show their bars.

The player who is closest to <u>1 whole bar</u> but not "over", wins 1 point.

The first player to get 4 points is the winner.

<u>Variation</u>

The player who is closest to 2 whole bars, but not "over", wins 2 points. The first player to get 8 points is the winner.

At first the students played this game by placing the shaded amounts of the bars end to end to determine the total shaded amount.

Gradually, this became unnecessary as the students became familiar with the bars. Mike and Alex revised **Fraction Bar Black Jack** (see illustration) by requiring that three arbitrary fraction bars be placed face up at the beginning of each round. The total shaded amount of these bars became the "target" for the round. They called their game **Super Black Jack.** In one round the following three bars were selected.

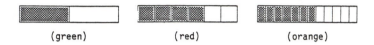

(green)   (red)   (orange)

Mike explained that the red bar can be combined with the green bar to form one whole bar with one part out of six left over. This can be put with the orange bar to give nine parts out of twelve. So for this round each player tried to get as close as possible to one whole bar and nine parts out of twelve. Alex won the round with the following four bars. He matched his red bar with the one on the board and put the left-over part of the red bar with his yellow bar to equal the shaded amount of the green bar. Then since one part out of four equals three parts out of twelve, he held with one whole bar and five parts out of twelve.

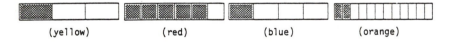

(yellow)   (red)   (blue)   (orange)

Every fraction bar has a corresponding playing card of the same color. When fraction numerals were introduced each student was supplied with a deck of fraction playing cards. The students usually combined their bars or cards to obtain a deck of 64 bars or 64 cards for a game. To help in sorting, the backs of each student's bars and cards were labeled with his or her initials.

There have been several memorable stories about students learning with the fraction bars. For example, shortly after the introduction of fraction numerals, one parent wanted to know if her son was learning about fractions by using the bars. The teacher asked the boy to deal out five fraction bars and find the smallest common denominator of the fractions. The boy gave both the smallest common denominator and the sum of the five fractions, while the parent was still trying to find the smallest common denominator. Needless to say, the parent went away satisfied.

One game which helps to provide a transition between the concrete (fraction bars) and abstract (fraction numerals) is called **Bars and Cards.**

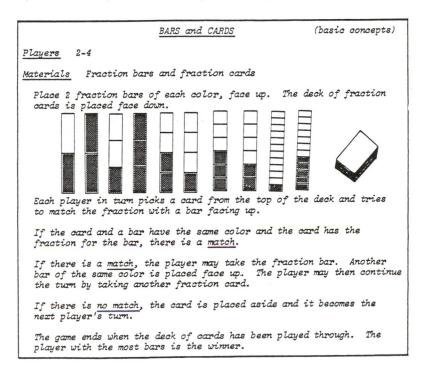

Over a period of several weeks, Mariana and Alexandra revised this game many times. They called their version **Super Bars and Cards.** Instead of placing 10 bars face up, each player is dealt five bars to be used only by that player. As in the original game, whenever a bar is won by a player another bar is put in its place. They created a discard pile of unused cards, which are placed face up. A player can now select a card from the deck or the discard pile. They also allowed equality and sums. That is, a player can win a bar if the fraction from the playing card equals the fraction from the bar; or, he or she can win several bars if the sum of the fractions for the bars equals the fraction on the card. If a player used a card from the discard pile to win one or more bars, he or she can continue playing by taking another card from either the deck or the discard pile. But if the player selects a card from the deck, he or she cannot take another card on that turn. When all the cards in the deck have been used, the discard pile is turned over and used as the deck. The game continues until all the bars have

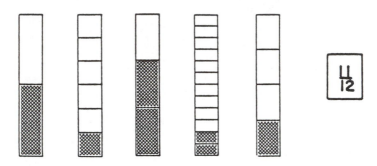

been won or no more plays are possible. At one time Alexandra had these bars, and turned over a playing card with $^{11}\!/_{12}$. She won two bars by combining the $\frac{2}{3}$ bar and the $\frac{1}{4}$ bar to get $^{11}\!/_{12}$. How could she have won three bars?

Many of the published games which were designed for fraction bars were changed by the students so that they could be played with both the bars and cards. The next game is described with fraction bars, and the students' version shows how fraction playing cards were brought into the game.[2]

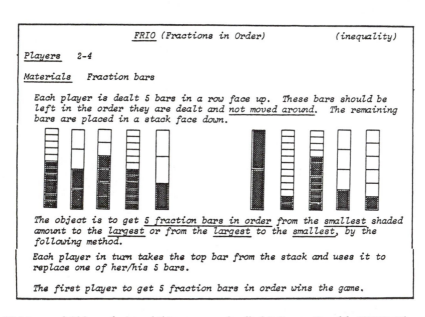

Kristan and Abby redesigned this game and called it **Super Double FRIO.** They allow each player to rearrange her or his bars to obtain an increasing or decreasing sequence of fractions. However, to win the game the difference between any two adjacent fractions must be $\frac{1}{2}$. Their game uses the bars and fraction playing cards which are both placed face down in separate decks.

On a player's turn he or she may select a bar or card. If a bar is chosen it may be used to replace any of the player's bars, as in the original game. But if a card is chosen it may be placed to the left or right of any bar, and any of the five bars may be removed. For example, Abby had the five bars shown below and selected a playing card with $\frac{9}{12}$. She put the $\frac{9}{12}$ card between the $\frac{4}{6}$ bar and the $\frac{10}{12}$ bar to obtain three fractions in order, and removed the $\frac{1}{4}$ bar.

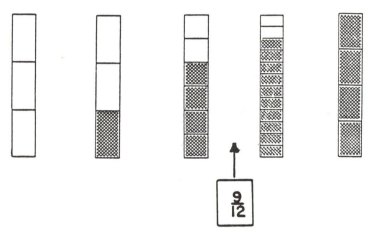

Since the bars and cards are colored (halves green, thirds yellow, fourths blue, sixths red, and twelfths orange), a player always knows the denominator of the fraction on the top bar or card in a deck. Therefore, a player's strategy may be to choose a bar rather than a card depending on the fraction that is needed. In a later revision of this game the students placed the unused bars face up in a discard pile and the unused cards face up in a discard pile. On a player's turn, he or she can select a bar or card from the two decks or two discard piles. The first player to obtain five fractions in order wins the game.

The preceding games are only a few of those which were revised or created by the students. Seth and Jason created **Super Concentration** when Seth was teaching Jason the **Addition Game.** Heather and Tosca created **Super Rummy** in which a player tries to obtain runs of three or more "consecutive" fractions which increase by either twelfths, sixths, fourths, thirds, or halves. Alie, Amy, Chikayo, and Jenny invented a game called **Two Run.**

Several students organized tournaments for some of the games. Alex and Billy set up a tournament for **Number Line Racing.** The Equality Race tournament which is shown below was organized and managed by Jon. In all the tournaments there was a winner's champion and loser's champion, and they competed for the class championship.

EQUALITY RACE

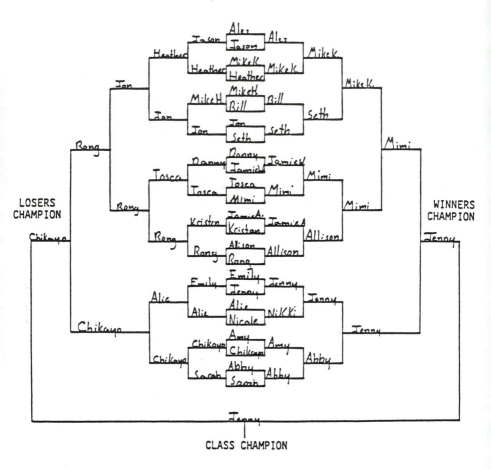

CLASS CHAMPION

Use of the Games

The fraction games are usually played in the students' spare time, after regular assignments have been completed. The readiness period for using the bars and playing the games should not be rushed. Preferably, the games should be played over several weeks rather than during a concentrated period. When fraction numerals are introduced, they will be used by students as a convenient notation for representing ideas with which they are familiar.

The fraction bar games and workbook are appropriate for grades 3 through 8. Many of the readiness games (before fraction numerals) have been used in grades 1 and 2. Joyce Strong, a first grade teacher at Oyster River Elementary School, has used several of these games with her students.

The fraction games have been used with a wide range of students, from learning disabled to gifted. One of the school's most severely handicapped learning disabled students had problems in processing and memory recall. According to tests which were given in earlier grades, this student was incapable of learning about fractions. However, the student eventually played most of the fraction bar games and successfully completed the workbook sections on basic concepts of a fraction and equality of fractions. Even students who are capable of computing with fractions can gain an understanding of fractions from visual experiences with the bars. These students not only have algorithms for using fractions, but they will be able to provide intuitive explanations. As examples, a student might explain that $\frac{1}{3} > \frac{1}{4}$ because when a bar is divided into 3 equal parts, the parts are bigger than when the bar is divided into 4 equal parts; or, that $\frac{1}{2} = \frac{2}{4}$ because if both parts of a $\frac{1}{2}$ bar are divided in half, there will be 4 parts and 2 shaded parts.

Conclusion

Several advantages have been gained from the combination of mathematical games and reading-writing instruction in the fifth grade class whose activities are described above. The emphasis on critical judgement and acceptance and promotion of student ideas resulted in an unusual amount of student initiative and creativity. The variety of published games provided the initial mathematical ideas which the students could easily learn, and then use in their games. In the process of creating and revising games, the students were involved in prewriting (creating new rules), writing (stating rules), and rewriting (making final adjustments). Perhaps of equal importance are the positive attitudes, as evidenced by the students' voluntary participation in the process of creating and revising new games, and their pride in sharing these games with others. The students' rewards were the challenges of developing better games and the recognition of having done so. Not only were the students peer teachers, teaching their games to other students, but they also taught their games to the teacher, student teacher, and teacher aide. By revising and creating games the students could begin to view rules as the results of human choices, and not as something fixed or authoritative. By proposing new rules and then playing the games and refining the rules, the students experienced the excitement of developing and evaluating their own ideas.

Albert B. Bennett, Jr. is Associate Professor of Mathematics at the University of New Hampshire. Peter Schiot is a fifth grade teacher at the Oyster River Elementary School in Durham, New Hampshire. For further information on fraction games, contact:

Albert B. Bennett, Jr.
Department of Mathematics
University of New Hampshire
Durham, NH 03824

or

Peter Schiot
Oyster River Elementary School
Durham, NH 03824

REFERENCES

Bennett, Jr., Albert B. and Patricia S. Davidson. 1973, 1981. **Fraction Bars.** Fort Collins, CO: Scott Resources, Inc.

Geeslin, William E. February 1977. "Using Writing About Mathematics as a Teaching Technique." **The Mathematics Teacher,** 70:112-115.

Graves, Donald H. 1983. **Writing: Teachers and Children At Work.** Exeter, NH: Heinemann Educational Books.

Shaw, Joan G. May 1983. "Mathematics Students Have a Right to Write." **The Arithmetic Teacher,** 30:16-18.

END NOTES

[1]These games are from Bennett, Jr., A.B., **Fraction Bars Step By Step Teacher's Guide** (Fort Collins, CO: Scott Resources, Inc. 1973)

[2]FRIO was first described by Rowena Drizigacker, **Arithmetic Teacher,** Vol. 6, No. 4, December 1966, 436-37.

WORD PROBLEMS
FOR KIDS BY KIDS

by Susan Larkin

The teacher explains a math concept, and the students practice. Elementary math texts provide plenty of exercises for students learning to add, subtract, multiply, and divide, but do they provide enough practice for students learning to solve word problems? Following is a typical encounter. I say to a fourth grader in my class, "You are in a store. You pick up a basketball that costs $7.50, a baseball mitt that costs $10.48, and a hockey stick that costs $12.32. You take these items to the cashier. How can you figure out how much you owe?" The child answers, "Subtract?"

The method that I see children using when they try a word problem is to look at the problem, grab any numbers available, pick an operation out of a hat, and hope it comes out right. Math books provide plenty of practice pages for a student learning to add, subtract, multiply, or divide, but very little practice for a student learning to apply these skills. Children ask, when they start a page of word problems, "Are these all minus?" My answer has always been, "Why don't you read each problem carefully and figure out what it's asking?"

It seems to me that the problem pages in math textbooks are often too abstract. They are often grown-up problems that the children can't understand. In the past I have tried using extra pages of problems for more practice, but most of these pages are not much different from the problems in the regular math book.

This past school year I made a resolution to do everything I could to make my math program as effective as it could possibly be. I always drill my fourth graders on multiplication facts until I think they have been mastered, but this year I continued the drill daily throughout the year. Every day we took a three-minute test that had fifty facts—addition, subtraction, multiplication, division, or mixed. If any student could finish before I did and get 100%, he or she would be exempt from the test in the future. We all improved. Every day there also was a regular math lesson and assignment on the current chapter. Most days there was an "easy" math assignment on something such as time, change, Roman numerals, etc.

I thought that students were making good progress until one day a page of math problems was assigned. I told the class that with so much recent practice, I expected they would find the twelve problems easy. A sticker would be awarded to every perfect paper. As I corrected the papers, I was devastated. The scores were horrible! What good was all this math practice if the students couldn't use it?

TEACHING MATHEMATICS

The very next weekend I decided to sit down at our home computer, a Macintosh, and write some math problems for extra practice. I wrote about a situation familiar to most students. Following is my first attempt at writing a problem page:

Toys!

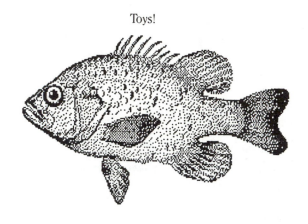

1. _____ walked into Kaybee Toys with a ten dollar
   Write your name here
   bill. _____ saw a model that _____ wanted for $5.32.
   write He or She
   _____ also saw a GoBot for $2.21. On _____ way out
   _____ saw a box of stickers for $1.23. Did _____ have enough
   money for all three of these items?

2. To figure the sales tax on these toys, you have to multiply the total by .07. What was the sales tax on these toys?

3. What was the total amount of money needed for the toys plus the sales tax?

4. Did _____ get any change?

5. If _____ got change, how much was it?

I showed this page to my son, David, who is in fifth grade, and asked him what he thought of it. He said that if he were writing problems, he would leave out the blanks because kids wouldn't want to fill them in. He said he would use the pronoun, you, instead. Taking his advice I wrote my second problem page, which follows.

Food

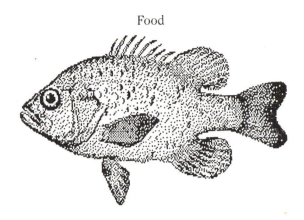

1. Your parents went to a fancy restaurant for dinner. They gave you $5.00 to go next door to Wendy's to get your own dinner. You decided to buy a bacon double cheeseburger for $1.75. You also wanted a Sprite for $.85 and a small order of french fries for $.75.

2. Restaurants charge sales tax on food. To compute the sales tax, multiply the total cost by .07. What was the sales tax on the food you wanted to buy? Did you have enough money for the food plus tax?

3. What was the total for the food plus the tax?

4. How much change did you receive?

5. Would you like a dessert?

6. If so, what dessert would you choose, and how much would it cost?

With the time I had left for weekend chores fast disappearing, I asked my son if he would write three more pages of word problems for me. I was determined to give my class daily practice in this obviously weak area. With some coaxing and an offer of payment for each page completed, my son took over the job. Following is one of his first pages. The fish, a picture found in the scrapbook that comes with the Macintosh, was obviously just for decoration. It had no relationship to the problems.

Stickers

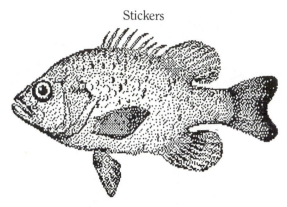

1. You want to buy a big package of stickers for $5.00. You mow the lawn for $.75, you find $1.00 lying on the ground, and you clean your smelly old basement for $2.75. You also find two quarters, three dimes, three nickels, and five pennies under your doghouse. Do you have enough money to buy these stickers?

2. You give all your change to your mom and she gives you back an equal amount of money in dollar bills. What will the sales tax be? To find the sales tax, multiply .07 by the amount of money you're spending.

3. You go to your favorite toy store and buy the wonderful stickers. How much money, if any, will you have left?

4. Do you want to stick a sticker on your dog's nose?

5. Do you want to put the rest on your fridge, or put them in your sticker book?

I copied these pages at school and presented one each day to my class. I read the problems, we discussed questions, worked out answers independently, and went over them together. Each lesson took about fifteen minutes and the children enjoyed them, probably because the problems were about kids and were sometimes funny. I decided to add this daily practice to my math schedule, which meant that each weekend David or I would have to write more problems. The format remained pretty much the same, five to eight paragraphs on a page, some asking math questions, some just listing facts, and some asking questions having nothing to do with math. I think such a setup discouraged kids from just grabbing numbers and guessing at an operation. Some "problems" weren't even problems! Not every decision made in life requires an answer to a mathematical question. My intention was to write about situations that were more realistic than some of those described in math books.

We continued the project for a few weeks, using pictures for decoration. We bought a disk called MacPic which contained nothing but pictures, so we didn't have to use the fish at the top of every page. David, even with monetary compensation, eventually grew tired of writing problems every weekend. If the project were to continue, I was going to have to write some more problems. Looking at the pictures we had, I decided to relate my problems to the picture at the top of the page. I wrote one series of problems dealing with money. Following is one such page.

1. Your parents give you a dollar. You walk to the candy store to buy some treats. You decide to buy 5 gumballs for $.05 each, 4 licorice sticks for $.08 each, and one Sugar Daddy for $.38. How much change do you get?

2. You eat all the candy and get several toothaches. Your mother calls the dentist and makes an appointment for you. She calls at 10:00 a.m. She tells you that the appointment is at 3:15 on the same day she calls. How long do you have to wait before your appointment?

3. While waiting for your dentist appointment you go to the town library. You check out 8 books. You weigh yourself and the books at the drug store. You and the books weigh 98 pounds. After you put the books down your weight drops to 85 pounds. How much do the books weigh?

4. While at the drug store, you (who apparently didn't learn anything from your last candy experience) use your last nickel to buy three pieces of bubble gum. If each piece costs a penny, how much change, if any, do you receive?

5. The dentist finds four cavities in your candy-infested teeth. She tells you that she will fill the cavities at a cost to your parents of $15.00 per cavity. How much will your cavity fillings be?

6. The dentist says you can have pain-killing novocaine for $2.00 extra. You call your mother. She says you can have the novocaine if you pay the $2.00 out of your next week's allowance. Which do you choose: pain and allowance, or no pain and no allowance?

As you can see, I had a good time on this one, including as many different kinds of operations as I could, along with a small lesson on the dangers of tooth decay. My inspirations, however, didn't last long. I was running out of ideas. If I can write problems, I thought, and my son can write problems, why can't the students in my class write problems? I made copies of the pictures we had in MacPic, and later in MacPic II, and posted them on a bulletin board. I offered my students 100 "tickets" for every problem page produced. These tickets could be used to play adventure games on the computer during recess. You needed 1,000 tickets for a half hour on the computer. A few students accepted the challenge and started writing problems. Each weekend David would type the pages that they wrote.

As students started seeing their own work "published," more and more of them began to write problems. Each day we would complete a problem sheet and either correct it together or the author would volunteer to correct the pages. Perfect papers received stickers. If we ever skipped doing problems, kids would ask why. They actually looked forward to solving math problems! Such daily practice was exactly what they needed.

As more and more students started writing problems, the project became a writing lesson as well as math practice. Some problems didn't make sense; some were too short for publication; and some needed work on capitalization and punctuation. I often handed problems back for editing before they were typed.

Some problems presented moral difficulties which I decided I had better "fix." One problem said that you did your brother's homework for money, and another said that if you earned enough money, your parents would allow you to punch your brother in the nose! When large amounts of money were "found," I added that you turned the money in to the police and waited the required amount of time to see if the owner showed up. Some pages were fairly realistic and some were off the wall, but all of them provided much needed practice.

Following are a few of the pages written by my students. The first is by a student whose work was always outstanding. Her problems, and she wrote many, were a joy to read. This project provided an opportunity to share the work of a gifted student.

Maple Syrup

1. You decide to make some maple syrup. You go to the library and get out a book on tapping trees. You go to your neighbors' and borrow the equipment. The next day you are in business! Your whole family wants to help. There are five of you, and there are 60 buckets. How many buckets do you each get to hang?

2. You tap 21 trees one day and 21 the next. How many trees do you tap in two days?

3. One day you get 30 quarts of sap, and 26 the next day. How much more sap did you get on the first day?

4. Your sap takes from 7:00 a.m. until 6:45 p.m. to boil down. Your sister's sap takes from 7:00 a.m. until 8:00 p.m. Your sister's fire isn't as big as yours is. How much longer does it take for your sister's sap to turn to syrup?

5. The next morning you have pancakes with maple syrup for breakfast. Do you want to make maple cream today?

The next page is by an above average student who also wrote many problems. He shared stories about track, football, fishing, and garage sales. His work, and those of the rest of my students, showed me that children know how to interest other children.

Football

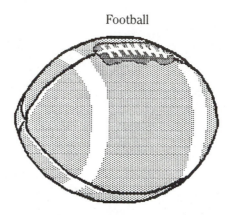

1. You are watching a football game when a player receives a kick on the 20 yard line. He runs to the 35 yard line but drops the ball. It rolls back 7 yards. He dives on the ball but can't go anywhere. How far is he from where he caught it?

2. The team moves the ball 3 yards on the first down, 5 yards on the second down, and 4 yards on the third down. Do they get a first down? Remember that a first down is 10 yards.

3. On the next four downs the team gets 6 yards on the first down, 5 yards on the second down, 8 yards on the third down, and 4 yards on the fourth down. However, they get a penalty and lose 15 yards. How far are they from where they started?

4. At the end of the game the score is 37 to 23. How many points did the victor win by?

5. On the way home with your parents, they stop at a store to buy some bread. You find out that it was 6 miles from the game to the store and it's 9 miles from the store to home. How far is it from the game to home?

The story about sailing, which follows, was written by an average student. He wrote several pages, many of which were fairly short. We often added problems when these pages were typed.

Sailing

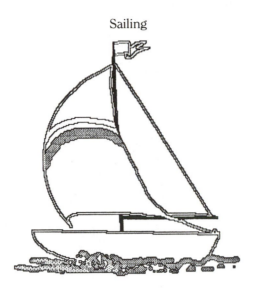

1. You want to go on a sailboat ride. It costs $3.00.

2. You get $1.00 for mowing the lawn. You get $.50 for getting a cat out of a tree. How much do you have?

3. Your mom gives you $1.50 for free. How much do you have now?

4. You go to the beach. Before you go on the sailboat ride, you get another $.50 for watching your little brother while your dad gets a soda. Do you have enough to buy yourself a pretzel and a soda? The pretzels are $.20 and the soda is $.40. You have to pay sales tax on pretzels and soda.

5. You leave for your sailboat ride at 10:45 a.m. You get back at 11:30 a.m. How long was your ride?

The last example is by a student who repeated fourth grade because of the large number of assignments not completed by the end of the year. He did write problem pages, though. Children love to have their work published.

A Trip To The Circus

1. You want to go to the circus. The tickets cost $5.00 each. You and your family are going (5 people, counting yourself). How much will 5 tickets cost?

2. Before you go to the circus, you ask your dad to stop at the flower shop to get some roses for the unicorn.

3. You buy a basket of 20 roses for $10.00. How many roses does everyone get to feed the unicorn?

4. When you get there, you look at your watch. It is 3:17, and the circus starts at 3:30. How early are you?

5. The circus is an hour and 30 minutes long. It is 4:30. How much longer will the show last?

6. When the circus is done, you go to the unicorn's stall and put the roses in it.

7. Do you want to ask the owner if you can go in the stall?

At the end of the year we decided to put all the pages together and make a book of math problems. Every student who contributed at least one page would get a copy of the book. When we finished in June, twenty-six of my twenty-seven students had contributed to the book. The book has over a hundred pages.

Pre-test and post-test data on BOCES CIMS test (New York's Board of Cooperative Education Services, Comprehensive Instructional Management System) indicate that my students improved more in problem-solving skills than did students in other fourth grade classes. Scores on math book problem pages also improved as our project continued. It would not be fair to say that these improvements were due only to our project. There are, of course, many other variables involved. I do think, though, that so much extra practice must have helped.

My emphasis always was for students to picture what was being asked for. When students are told to look for key words, the process loses meaning. They may know that "how many more" means subtract, but they don't know why.

In the future I probably will use the problems that we have already written at the beginning of the year and encourage students to write problems for their classmates. I would be happy to send a copy of our book to anyone who would like one, for the cost of copying it plus postage—namely $5.00.

I encourage other teachers to have their students make problem pages of their own. The Macintosh, of course, made the project much easier, but other computers have programs that provide scrapbooks. **Newsroom,** by Springboard Software, for example, includes over 600 pictures that can be printed. This program is available for both Apple II and the IBM PC. This project and past attempts at improving problem solving skills have convinced me that short, daily practice on story problems which kids can believe might happen to them will definitely improve mathematical thinking and reasoning skills. I think the project succeeds because the stories are interesting enough to attract the kids' attention, and the practice provided by answering similar types of questions over and over is definitely what many students need. If youngsters can be convinced that math skills are useful, they can be motivated to try to improve.

Susan Larkin taught fourth grade, and presently teaches remedial writing, at the Newark Valley Middle School in Brooktondale, New York. For further information on her word problems program, contact:

Susan Larkin
Box 107
Brooktondale, NY 14817

TEACHING STUDENTS TO THINK IN MATHEMATICS AND TO MAKE CONJECTURES

by Henry Borenson

"How many right angles does a rectangle have?" About half the class of fourth graders thought the correct answer was "four" and the other half thought it was "two." Before posing this question, I had already spent a minute or two verifying to my satisfaction that the students knew what a right angle was: they had pointed to the corner of the blackboard, the roof tiles, etc. And yet, the students were now giving me these two very different answers.

Knowing that there must be a rationale behind the students' answers, and wishing to emphasize the students' thinking, I took no position on the answers presented. Instead, I reported the two major answers to the class and asked for follow-up:

"Some students think the rectangle has four right angles and others think it has two. Who would like to come up to the blackboard to defend his or her position?" A girl's hand went up. "Here," I said, handing her the piece of chalk. She started to talk right away. I interrupted her: "First tell us what you think the answer is." "Two," she replied. "Now, tell us why," I added. Now everyone knew what position the girl was about to defend.

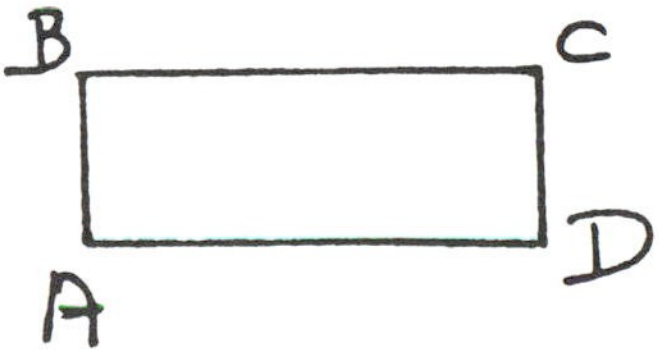

Her response was as follows: "The rectangle has two right angles, and they are the ones at C and D in the figure."

Figure 1

"All right," I said to the class, "what do you think now?" One girl raised her hand. Next thing I knew she was coming up to the blackboard. "What do you think?" I asked her. "It has four," was her reply. She then proceeded to point to the angles at C and D but also to the ones at A and B. Still being noncommittal, and being more a moderator than anything else, I asked the first girl what she thought about that (what the second girl had just said). The first girl was nonplused. She looked directly at me and replied, "Those [angles A and B] are left angles!" I, probably a bit apprehensively, now looked at the class and asked, "How many of you agree with her?" (that angles A and B are left angles). Now all the hands went up!! The class had reasoned it out and concluded that a rectangle has two right angles because the other two are "left angles!"

I had used the process I wanted to use, one of having the students logically defend their positions and arrive at the desired conclusion through consensus and understanding. This process, in the instance at hand, had led the class to a conclusion other than the one I wanted them to reach. I was pleased, at least, that my own position on the matter had been kept hidden so that the students could arrive at what, to them, was a logical conclusion.

At this point I had to think quickly so as to get myself and the students out of this predicament. I thought of one idea that might lead the students to reconsider the conclusion they had just arrived at. "Suppose I were a gymnast," I asked, "and I were looking at the rectangle from the top, which angles would be right angles now?"

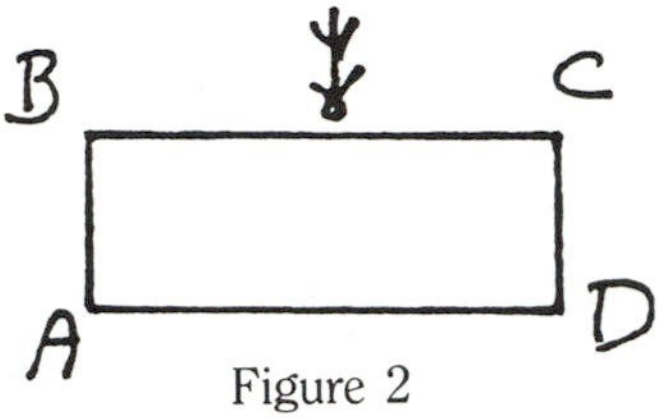

Figure 2

The students seemed to have no trouble "flipping" themselves over mentally and looking at the situation. A student I selected replied, "Two, A and B." "You mean," I said in dramatized astonishment, "that all left angles are really right angles?" There seemed to be a chorus of "yes" responses and I knew enough to quit at this point, stopping only to summarize, "We see, therefore, that a rectangle has four right angles."

Although no student offered the thought, it is possible that some of them may have concluded that a rectangle can equally be said to have four left angles. With time, the students would learn that these angles are always called right angles.

This incident is interesting because it illustrates a number of pedagogical elements which the teacher interested in developing student thinking in mathematics will frequently employ. The teacher in this incident did not see his major role as that of providing mathematical truths to his students for them to remember. The teacher was more interested in providing the setting wherein the students, through their own logical analysis and exploration, could arrive at the desired mathematical truths.

In the above example, the teacher demonstrated to his students that he valued and respected their thinking, their opinions, and their ability to reason mathematically. The teacher placed the emphasis on the mathematical process—not on the production of a "correct answer." The teacher was more interested in the defense which the students gave for the position they had taken, than on the position itself. Furthermore, the teacher was implicitly conveying to his students his expectation that they could verbalize their understanding of mathematics and that this verbalization was valued. Students as early as the primary grades are able to verbalize the rationale for their thinking and should be encouraged to do so.

Students who learn mathematics through the techniques suggested above will develop a sense of confidence and power in handling mathematics. They will learn that mathematics can be reasoned out and grasped in a meaningful way. Such students will tend to enjoy mathematics.

The teacher who employs the techniques suggested above will find that students, almost without exception, have a reason for thinking as they do. The teacher, with the help of the class, is then in a position to respond, not to the student's conclusions, but to the basis for those conclusions. Through this process, student errors in reasoning can be diagnosed and corrected at their source.

The techniques suggested also will encourage novel insights and student creativity. Take the following incident, for instance. In an eighth grade mathematics class, the students were asked if they thought any of the angles of a parallelogram are congruent.

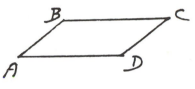

Figure 3

Renee raised her hand and said that angles A and C were congruent. "Tell us why you think so." "Those are alternate interior angles of parallel lines," the girl responded. At this point the teacher was in a state of disbelief: how could a student who had paid even the slightest attention to the class work come up with such a preposterous statement? The teacher began to wonder. The class had already done some work with alternate interior angles, such as angles 1 and 2 in figure 4.

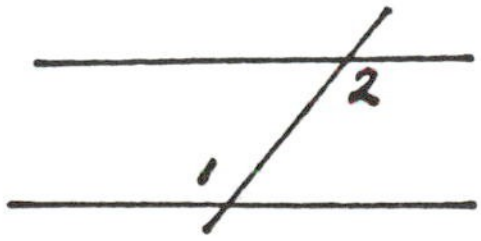

Figure 4

How could Renee make the kind of statement she did? The teacher, following the policy of encouraging students to defend their position, whatever it is, asked Renee to come up to the blackboard to show the class what she meant. (The teacher did this with a little trepidation for Renee, fearing that the class might laugh at her—even though such behavior had been strictly discouraged during the year.) "I don't have to come up," Renee said, "simply fold the parallelogram over so that $\overline{CD}$ lies on $\overline{AB}$."

The teacher hesitated for a second trying to comprehend what it was that Renee was saying. At this point some astonishment began to show on the teacher's face with the realization that

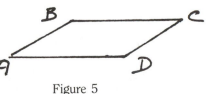

Figure 5

maybe there was something to what Renee was saying. The students in the class started to smile gleefully at the teacher's astonishment and in the realization that Renee, a fellow student, had evidently hit upon something creative.

The teacher then drew a large parallelogram on a piece of paper in front of the class, cut it out, rolled it over so that $\overline{CD}$ coincided with $\overline{AB}$ and then, lo and behold!, angles A and C were alternate interior angles of parallel lines!

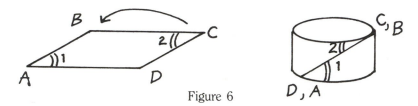

Figure 6

It had now been proven to the students and to the teacher that Renee was right! Her analysis was correct and logical, though at first it appeared as if she were way off base. Her novel argument demonstrated insight and skill at visualization— all of which would never have come to light if the teacher had not encouraged a student to defend the position she had taken, and if the teacher had not then attempted to understand that position.

Such moments do not occur every day. But they occur often enough in a teacher's career to be memorable, to add to the joy of teaching, and to add to the self-esteem of the students involved.

The teacher who sees the value of focusing on the process of mathematics and student comprehension will also want to encourage students to formulate mathematical conjectures. This may sound more complicated than it is.

A conjecture is nothing more than the statement of an observed generalization. After two or three instances of a phenomenon are noted, the student generalizes his/her observation. The process is referred to as inductive reasoning. A definition of inductive reasoning might be, "the process of arriving at a generalization on the basis of few, specific instances." The generalization arrived at through inductive reasoning is referred to as the conjecture. For example, in a fifth grade classroom, the students were asked to work examples such as 40×500, 30×50, and 200×40. Once the students were done, the teacher asked, "Does anyone notice a pattern?" Since no response was forthcoming, the teacher added, "Look at the answers carefully. Does anyone notice a way of doing the problems mentally?" A student suggested that the answer to 30×50 could be obtained by multiplying the 3 by the 5 and then adding the two zeroes. The teacher then posed this method to the class: "Let's see if Jerry's method works in the other cases," he said. After verifying the method in the remaining examples, the teacher asked, "How many of you think the method will work all the time?" Though most student hands went up, the teacher gave the class three additional examples on which to test Jerry's method. Finally, after the method was verified with these examples, the teacher highlighted the generalization by writing it on the board in the form of a conjecture, using the student's name:

"Jerry's Conjecture: To multiply two numbers, like 200×40, multiply the 2 by the 4 and then add the number of zeroes."

As another example, in a third grade classroom, the students were finding the areas of various rectangles on graph paper by counting the number of unit squares. The teacher asked if anyone had a shortcut. After a short pause, a student suggested that the answer could be obtained by multiplying the two numbers. The teacher then briefly defined "length," "width," and wrote the conjectures on the board as follows: "JoAnn's Conjecture: The area of any rectangle is equal to the length times the width." The teacher then provided the students with practice finding the areas of rectangles—practice in which the students could use JoAnn's Conjecture.

Students who are exposed to this process and encouraged to formulate conjectures will often be on the lookout for mathematical patterns and relationships—and will find many.

The teacher who values the inductive process of investigation will often find ways to assist students to discover the desired generalization or phenomenon. The following example illustrates this process of guided discovery. For instance, an eighth grade teacher wishes her students to discover that the measure of an inscribed angle of a circle is equal to one-half the measure of the intercepted arc.

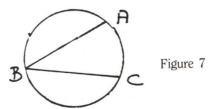

Figure 7

Goal: Have students discover mABC = ½ m$\widehat{AC}$

After defining the terms "inscribed angle" and "intercepted arc," the teacher can pose the following questions to the class: "I wonder if there is a relationship between the measure of the inscribed angle and the measure of the intercepted arc. How can we find out?" Students may suggest fruitful paths for investigation.

67

If none are forthcoming, the teacher might proceed as follows: "Well, maybe we can find the answers for special cases and see if we can notice a pattern. Consider the two cases which follow."

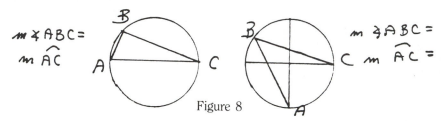

$m \sphericalangle ABC =$

$m \overset{\frown}{AC}$

$m \sphericalangle ABC =$

$m \overset{\frown}{AC} =$

Figure 8

(Since we are investigating, we do not want the figures to mislead us: therefore, the figures should be drawn with compass and straight edge. It is preferable if the students draw their own figures and investigate further before classroom discussion resumes.)

The students will conclude that, in the first figure, $\sphericalangle ABC$ is a right angle and $m\overset{\frown}{AC}$ is 180. By measuring the angle in figure 2 with a protractor, the students will get $m \sphericalangle B \approx 45$. Also $m\overset{\frown}{AC}=90$, since it is half of a semicircle. With this information, someone in the class will suggest the relationship existing between the inscribed angle and the intercepted arc. This relationship should then be written on the board as a conjecture, with the student's name attached, for the class to copy. The teacher then can give the class examples in which to apply the conjecture.

Through the above process, the teacher has succeeded in leading the students to develop as a conjecture the desired mathematical property which she wants them to learn. The students have become active participants in developing mathematics rather than passive recipients of someone else's mathematical conclusions.

Sometimes, of course, student conjectures may be false. The following incident illustrates how one teacher handled a student's false conjecture. In a seventh grade mathematics classroom, the students were studying ways in which two triangles could be shown to be congruent. The students had just learned that if the three sides of one triangle are congruent to the three sides of a second triangle, then the two triangles are congruent. The teacher asked, "Are there any other ways in which two triangles could be shown to be congruent?" John suggested that if the three angles of one triangle are congruent to the three angles of the second triangle, then the two triangles are congruent. "How many of you think that's true?" the teacher asked, thus placing the conjecture for consideration by the class. Most hands went up. "Do any of you think it's not true?" Now three hands went up. "Who would like to come up to the board to present his or her ideas to the class?" A student volunteered. She came up to the board, drew the two triangles in figure 9, and said, "The angles of these two triangles are congruent, but the triangles themselves are not congruent." The teacher thanked the student and

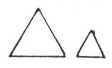

Figure 9

then asked the class, "What do you think about that?" As he did so, he surveyed the class, including the student who made the original proposition. "John?" John smiled and nodded—it was now clear to him that his proposition could not be maintained. John had been presented with a counterexample, and so he reassessed his own position. "Can someone summarize what we've learned?" the teacher asked. A student volunteered that we could not be sure that two triangles are congruent just because their angles are congruent.

In the above example, the teacher knew at once that John's proposition was false. Yet, he tried to avoid giving any signs, verbally or nonverbally, that it was a false proposition. The teacher's intent was to have the class consider the mathematical idea proposed by John on its own merits. As in this case, classmates frequently are able to come up with a counterexample that invalidates a false conjecture. As in this illustration, the whole interaction can be carried out in a positive, constructive, and supportive environment—an environment which does credit to the scientific process of investigation.

Of course, if the class cannot make progress with a proposition, it is perfectly fine for the teacher to guide the class toward the desired conclusion. For instance, in the example just described, the teacher could have drawn the two triangles on the board,

Figure 10

and asked, "Is it possible for these triangles to have congruent angles?" "Are the triangles congruent?" Such questions would help the class to arrive at the desired conclusion. Students see such an approach by the teacher as one which treats their conjectures with respect. It encourages students to risk proposing other conjectures in the future.

In summary, focusing on mathematics as a thinking process, by encouraging students to defend their mathematical positions, and by helping students to formulate conjectures, teachers will appreciably enhance the quality of mathematics education in their classrooms. In particular, teachers will help students

- develop a sense of power in mathematics that makes them more comfortable in handling new mathematical situations
- develop the ability to verbalize their mathematical thinking
- learn mathematics in a meaningful and refreshing way.

At the same time, the teacher will be obtaining continuous, ongoing feedback on the extent of students' understanding, thus allowing early diagnosis of errors in student thinking. Finally, the teacher will experience a sense of professional pride in seeing the students engaged in a process of meaningful and rewarding learning.

Henry Borenson is the District Mathematics Coordinator for the Council Rock School District in Richboro, Pennsylvania and a teacher in the district. For further information on his mathematics program, contact:

Henry Borenson, Ed.D.
1469 Neshaminy Valley Drive
Bensalem, PA 19020

LOGO: A TOOL FOR TEACHING MATHEMATICAL FLEXIBILITY

by Alan Lipp

Modern cognitive science is producing a new paradigm for understanding how we learn mathematics; and this new paradigm has powerful implications as to how mathematics should be taught.

We are coming to see knowledge in general, and mathematical knowledge in particular, as being actively constructed by the learner. That is, the learner is a participant in making mathematics meaningful. It is no longer possible to justify the position that if we "pour enough mathematical facts" into our students that they will begin to "think like mathematicians" (Seymour Papert, **Mindstorms**). Rather, from the outset, we must make mathematics meaningful both to ourselves and to our students.

One method which encourages going beyond the immediate facts is to look for more than one solution to a problem. Discovering multiple solutions requires fluency in the production of mathematical ideas. LOGO can be a useful tool in developing mathematical fluency.

For example, rather than asking a student to write a procedure for drawing a rectangle, consider the more provoking question: Find 3 different LOGO procedures which will draw a rectangle.

Possible solutions include:

```
TO RECTANGLE 1:A :B
REPEAT 2 FD :A RT 90 FD :B RT 90
END

TO RECTANGLE2 :A :B

SETXY 0 :A
SETXY :A :B
SETXY :B 0
SETXY 0 0
END
```

```
TO RECTANGLE3 :A :B          where          TO EL :X
EL :A                                        FD :X RT 90
EL :B                                        END
EL :A
EL :B
END
```

Of course, there are many other possible solutions! The important consideration is that the procedures above are not the "right answers." There are right and wrong answers—but the criterion for judging the correctness of a student's answer is whether or not the procedure produces a rectangle, not whether the student has figured out the answer in the back of the book.

A major goal in teaching LOGO is to help students formulate the concept of subprocedures interacting. A related goal is to help students to visualize geometric events more dynamically, to be able to break up a given geometric object into sub-objects in different (and appropriate) ways. An analogy with rubber stamps may be useful to encourage both kinds of concept development.

By a rubber stamp I mean a printing stamp complete with ink pad; only our stamps will have, instead of messages or signatures, geometric objects. Suppose we have a supply of "line stamps" in various lengths. The stamp Line-1 gives a line segment one unit long; Line-2 gives a segment two units long, etc.

We pose the question, "How can we print a rectangle whose dimensions are 1×1?" Clearly, with our stamps we can do this in only one way, by making four impressions with the Line-1 stamp turned 90 degrees each time. Next: "How can we print a rectangle whose dimensions are 1×2?"

Now we have two options. Either do all printing with Line-1 or two prints with Line-1 and two with Line-2. Which is better? For our purposes it is the act of noticing that the rectangle can be completed in more than one way that is crucial. But we may note for the record that one method requires six impressions with a single stamp while the second requires only four impressions but we must use two different stamps.

What about a 2×3 rectangle? The options multiply rapidly. We can use the Line-1 stamp (10 impressions), or the Line-1 and Line-2 stamps, or Line-1 and Line-3, or Line-2 and Line-3.

The number of possibilities is already rich enough to pose several interesting questions. Using the Line-1 and Line-2 stamps, in how many different ways can we create our 2×3 rectangle?.

Suppose we do not have an unlimited number of stamps, perhaps we have just the Line-2 and Line-3 stamps. Can we construct a 4×15 rectangle? Are there rectangles that we cannot construct? Can we characterize those rectangles which can be constructed and those which cannot?

An L Stamp
Figure 1

A Reversed L
Figure 2

We need not restrict ourselves to segments. Suppose we have available "L" shaped stamps (figure 1). For example, a stamp which produces an "L" with a height of 3 and a width of 1. Can we use just our L-stamp to construct a square? Can we construct a nonsquare rectangle? If we have both an "L" and a reversed "L" (figure 2), what size rectangle can we construct? If our "L" (and reversed "L") have heights of :A and widths of :B, what size squares and rectangles can we construct? What is the sequence in which we must use our stamps to produce a rectangle?

The solutions to each of these problems require the visual disassembling of the rectangle into sub-objects, ELs and LEs (reversed ELs), and the construction of appropriate impression sequences for producing the desired figures.

An open-ended exploration involving these figures might encourage learners to see what designs they can construct using these "L" shapes. This constructive work requires learners to actively engage the knowledge they are trying to use and not merely to possibly reproduce standard answers to textbook questions.

Explorations in LOGO can play an important part in the development of the fluency and flexibility of thought we wish to encourage in our students to help them to construct meaningful mathematics.

TEACHING MATHEMATICS

Alan Lipp is the Computer Coordinator for SummerMath, Mt. Holyoke College, and also Director of Academic Computing at Williston Northampton School in Easthampton, Massachusetts. In addition to teaching mathematics, he presents training workshops to both teachers and students. For further information on his use of LOGO in teaching mathematics, contact:

Alan Lipp
280 North Main Street
South Deerfield, MA 01373

REAL WORLD HELP FOR THE MIDDLE GRADES MATHEMATICS CLASSROOM

by Murray Siegel

Much attention has been paid to the teaching of mathematics in secondary schools. It is obvious that the high school student must be prepared for the mathematical realities of being a consumer and wage earner. It is also apparent that the high school student must be ready for the mathematical requirements of college. Focus has similarly been placed on the teaching of mathematics in the primary grades. The need to create a sound foundation in the early grades is evident to anyone concerned with the development of mathematical ability in our young people.

The one area which has not drawn significant attention is the middle grades. Yet in sixth, seventh, and eighth grades, mathematical concepts and methods vital to later success are introduced and reinforced. It is in the middle grades where "math anxiety" begins to grow. The anxiety eventually leads a large percentage of our citizenry to be cut off from mathematical learning.

Many of the concepts developed in the middle grades are difficult for the student to assimilate. Thus, we are forced to repeat the teaching of many areas within the curriculum at each grade level. This is especially true for the arithmetic of fractions and the use of percentages. A perusal of many textbook series will reveal that the texts for the sixth, seventh, and eighth grades are quite similar. The types of problems vary little and the level of difficulty increases at a rather small rate from grade to grade.

The students need the repetition but they do recognize that they have "learned this stuff last year." Unfortunately they have forgotten much of what they learned last year. The lessons can become tedious for the students and frustrating for the concerned teacher. A point is reached where the concepts are deemed by the students to be too difficult to ever grasp. Ultimately, the students question the reasons for their being forced to learn this unnecessary material.

This article is an attempt to help middle grades teachers who seek new ideas for mathematical lessons. In it, I make suggestions designed to present mathematics that students should find interesting. The lessons have been selected to allow the teacher to demonstrate the usefulness of the mathematics being taught, in the real world. Furthermore, to bring the suggestions in line with existing curricula, units of the mathematics curriculum taught in the middle grades have been identified and specific real world uses of the mathematics in each unit are stated.

An alphabetical list of each real world use is provided with appropriate explanations.

The real-world applications offered here relate to probability and statistics, which is one area that most teachers, including many math teachers, avoid because of negative experiences in statistics classes in college. However, the graphical and computational techniques described involve no Greek letters and no abstract symbol manipulation. In fact, the real world uses are simply practical applications to be included in the existing curriculum to enhance the learning of mathematics at this critical time in a student's academic life.

I realized the value of statistics in the teaching of middle grades math a number of years ago when I was having difficulty teaching percents in an eighth grade pre-algebra class. I organized the class into groups, and each group surveyed the local community's knowledge of the order of presidential succession. This was a short time after Nixon's resignation and the subject of who was next in line was very topical. Because the students were dealing with the numbers that had meaning to them (since they had collected the data), they seemed to be more interested in the mathematics. Each group determined the fraction of its sample that had the correct answer for each question. Each fraction was converted to a percentage and the percentages were graphed. A long discussion took place in class about the use of percentages in comparing the results for each group. The students understood why percents were useful and retained the technique for converting a fraction to a decimal to a greater extent than other classes who had used standard textbook problems.

Through this project, I had made the discovery that there were two types of statistics: the college type that so often seems meaningless and the real world type that had aided me in the teaching of mathematics. I began to look for ways to use statistical topics to aid in the presentation of my subject matter. I found remedial classes were interested in adding and multiplying fractions when they knew that they needed these skills to compute probabilities and odds in "gambling" situations. Division with rounding off became less painful when used to find the average rating of a movie or popular rock group after students had gathered the data themselves. Coordinate plotting made more sense to seventh graders when they were plotting points which represented data that they had gathered to see if there was a relationship between shoe size and family size. The use of "X" as a symbol to stand for a measurement presented no problem for sixth graders and gave them a better feeling for the meaning of the word "variable."

Eventually I found time in my fifth, sixth, and seventh grade curriculum for a complete unit on statistics. This unit tied together all the mathematics the students had learned to date and emphasized the use of calculators and our microcomputer. I have taught mathematics from fifth grade to graduate school and to students who varied in ability from remedial to gifted. In all cases, where I could use statistical topics, I found that the use of live data collected by students and the use of various computational and graphical techniques on these data enhanced my ability to teach arithmetic, algebra, and calculus.

I firmly believe, based on my experience in the classroom, that the material I have put together and described here can be beneficial to the middle grades student and teacher.

Table I

MATH UNIT	REAL WORLD USE
use of counting numbers	mode median frequency distributions rating systems stem and leaf plots random number table
long division (including rounding off)	mean
definition of fraction	probability
ratios	odds
adding fractions	probability of an OR situation sum of probabilities
subtracting fractions	missing probability complementary events
multiplying fractions	probability of an AND situation expectation
dividing fractions	odds
meaning of percent	ratings, polls, and surveys

fraction↔%	estimating population proportions from sample data percentiles quartiles theoretical probability
percent problems	ratings, polls, and surveys
graphing	histogram relative frequency histogram frequency polygon box plot
coordinate plotting	scatter plot
angle measurement	circle graph
slope	eyeball fit line median fit line predictions
use of variable	frequency distribution scatter plot predictions
reading charts, tables and graphs	histogram frequency distribution frequency polygon circle graph random number plot stem and leaf plot box plot scatter plot
estimation	estimating the mean from a histogram estimating the mean from a frequency distribution bias

My collection of middle-school statistics activities includes the following topics, listed alphabetically. This is a partial list of topic descriptions. For a more complete list, you may contact me. Words in boldface in the explanations represent uses from the real world, as listed in Table I.

Bias: Can the average height of the students in the school be obtained by measuring the boys' basketball team, a sample of twenty-five seniors, or a sample of one hundred female students. In each case the answer is "no" since the sample is not representative of all the students in the school. Selecting a sample that is not representative of the population introduces bias into the results. For an exercise, have the students estimate some average (height, time, number of hours of TV watched, etc.) for a general population. Then give possible numerical values for this average that vary from the class's expectations. Have students explain possible reasons for the difference.

Circle Graph: There is a graph where the **relative frequency** of the outcome is represented by the size of its segment of the circle. That is, if 25% of the sample chose "red" then the portion of the circle which was labeled "red" would be one-fourth of the total circle (or 90 degrees). The angle is obtained by multiplying $360°$ by the relative frequency.

Estimating Population Proportions From Sample Data: In a sample of twenty-five people, four watch NBC News, seven watch ABC News, ten watch CBS News, three watch CNN News, and one person watches no TV news. We can estimate the proportion of the population that watches a particular network's news (as a percent) by converting the fraction of the sample that watches that network's news to a percent.

NBC	$4/25 \times 100/1 = 16\%$
ABC	$7/25 \times 100/1 = 28\%$
CBS	$10/25 \times 100/1 = 40\%$
CNN	$3/25 \times 100/1 = 12\%$
no TV news	$1/25 \times 100/1 = 4\%$

Expectations: I am going to flip a fair coin (50% chance of heads) 10 times. How many heads do you expect? Then have each student flip a coin ten times. Compute the **mean** of the number of heads. How did it match your expectations? If I select one hundred telephone numbers from a randomly selected page in the telephone book (white pages), what do you expect the mean value to be for the last digit of one hundred numbers? Each student computes the mean of his or her one hundred digits and the class discusses the validity of the expectation. How about the mean of the means (add up each student's mean and divide by the number of students)?

Eyeball Fit Line: For a given set of paired data, the student constructs a **scatter plot.** Now draw a straight line that best approximates the pattern of the dots (most of the dots are fairly close to the line). The accuracy of the "eyeball fit" is not vital. Now select two points on the line and compute the slope (see figure 1). This means that for every increase of one unit for the X (horizontal) measurement we expect the Y (vertical) measurement to increase by two.

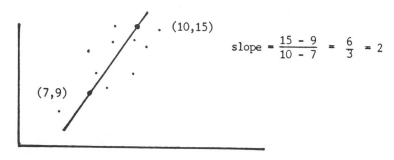

$$\text{slope} = \frac{15 - 9}{10 - 7} = \frac{6}{3} = 2$$

Figure 1

Frequency Distribution: If I take a sample by measuring students' heights to the nearest inch, the frequency of a measurement is the number of times it occurs. For example:

measurement	frequency
54	8
56	12
57	10
59	7
60	3
61	1
67	1
	42

The frequency of 57″ is 10. The table showing the measurements in ascending order and their frequencies is called a frequency distribution. Note that the sum of the frequencies is the number of students in the sample (called the sample size).

Figure 2

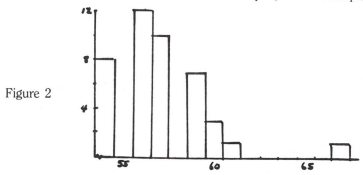

Histogram: This is a bar graph of the **frequency distribution.** Use the example given in defining the frequency distribution (see figure 2).

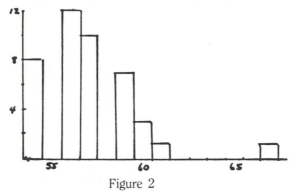

Figure 2

Mean: The precise term for what we usually call the average is the **mean.** The **mode** and **median** are other forms of averages. The mean is obtained by adding up all the measurements and dividing by the number of measurements (the sample size). If a **frequency distribution** is available, one can obtain the sum of all measurements by multiplying each measurement by its frequency. The sum of these products is the sum of all the measurements. Note that the sample size is available when using the frequency distribution (the sum of the frequency column). The symbol for the mean is $\overline{X}$ (X-bar). As example:

measurement	frequency	frequency×measurement	
2	3	6	
3	7	21	
4	10	40	$\overline{X}=116/29=4$
5	7	35	
7	2	14	

Through such examples, students come to realize that the mean does not always work out to be a whole number. The answer could be left as a mixed number $128/29=4\ 12/29$ or rounded off to whatever place value you wish. So, $143/15=9.5333\ldots$ or 10 (rounded to a whole number) or 9.5 or 9.53, etc.

Median: This is the measurement found in the middle of a set of data if the data are put in order. If the sample size is an odd number then there is a distinct middle measurement. If the number of measurements in the sample is an even number then the median is the **mean** of the two measurements in the middle 7, 7, 8, 9, 9, 9, **10**, 10, 11, 12, 12, 13, 17. Since there are 13 measurements, the measurement in the middle is the seventh one which is 10. Thus the median (md) is 10. 1, 3, 4, 4, **4, 5,** 5, 6, 6, 6. Since there are 10 measurements, the two in the middle are the fifth and sixth which are 4 and 5. The mean of 4 and 5 is 4.5 (4+5)/2.

The median is useful as an average for data that contain a small number of highly divergent numbers. The mean is affected greatly by divergent data, the median is not. The average family income or the average price of a new home would be stated using a median. For example, 7, 8, 9, 10, 11. The mean and median are both 9. If 100 is added so that the data are 7, 8, 9, 10, 11, 100 then the mean jumps to 24.17 while the median changes to 9.5.

Median Fit Line: Given a **scatter plot,** one can drawn a line that approximates the points by using an **eyeball fit** or by using a median fit line. Draw two vertical lines which divide the points into three approximately equal groups. The lines should not go through any of the scatter points (see figure 1). Note: the "2" means that there are two people who are represented by the same point. Thus the scatter points are divided into groups of 5, 5, and 6. Find the **median** value of X and the median value of Y for each group. For each group plot the point Xm, Ym where Xm is the median value of X for that group and Ym is the median value of Y for that group. Draw a small X at each of these three points.

Lightly draw a line between the X for the first group and the X for the third group. Then slide your ruler so that it's one-third of the distance between this line and the X for the second group. Draw a line here that is parallel to the first line. This is the median fit line. You can now examine the slope of the median fit line to see how much Y changes if X is changed.

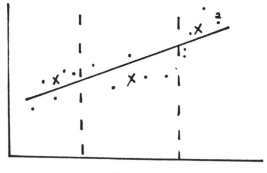

Figure 3

Percentiles: A percentile indicates the percentage of all the measurements that are less than or equal to the measurement in question. For example, given the following **frequency distribution,** percentiles can be determined.

measurement	frequency
2	3
4	5
5	6
7	3
8	2
10	1

The percentile for the measurement 7, for example, is found by counting the number of measurements at or below 7. There are 17 (3+5+6+3). Since there are 20 measurements, 17/20 of the measurements are less than or equal to 7. Thus: 17/20×100/1=85%. So, 7 is at the 85th percentile.

Predictions: In statistics we are seeking to make accurate predictions of one measurement using a readily available measurement. For example, we might try to estimate a male's adult height by using his length at birth. This estimating formula is written as an equation. How this equation is obtained is called regression analysis which is beyond the scope of this article. So, given an estimating equation: y=2x+30 where y is the male's adult height and x is the length at birth. If a male baby is 22 inches at birth then we predict that his adult height will be 2 (22) + 30 = 74 or 6′2″.

Probability: Probability is the chance of an event happening. A probability of 0 means that the event cannot happen. A probability of 1 means that you are certain that the event will occur. All other probabilities are proper fractions, defined by:

Probability of an event A = $\dfrac{\text{\# outcomes which are A}}{\text{total number of outcomes}}$

Examples: There are 6 outcomes if you roll a die—1, 2, 3, 4, 5, and 6. The probability of rolling an odd number is 1/2 since the number of outcomes which are odd is 3 and 3/6=1/2.

Given the following **frequency distribution,**

measurement	frequency
3	2
4	5
6	8
7	4
10	3

the probability of a person's measurement being more than 6 is 7/22 since there are 7 outcomes that are greater than 6 and the total number of outcomes is 22.

Quartiles: Quartiles use the 25th, 50th, and 75th **percentiles.** A person is said to be in the 1st quartile if his measurement is at or below the 25th percentile, etc. Given the following measurements,

2, 4, 5, 5, 6, 7, 8, 8, 8, 9, 11, 15

the 25th percentile or 1st quartile is at 5 since 1/4 (25%) of all measurements are at or below 5.

$$25\% = 1/4 = ?/12, \ ? = 3$$

Since the third measurement is 5, the 25th percentile is at 5. The second quartile ends at 7 (50th percentile) since 6/12=1/2=50% and 6 measurements are at or below 7. The third quartile ends at 8 since 9/12=3/4=75% and 9 of the 12 measurements are at or below 8. Many colleges will only consider applications of students who are in the top quartile of their senior class. These students are, therefore, above the 75th percentile.

Rating System: A rating system simply awards a numerical score as a rating. The score should be a counting number within a given range of numbers. A higher number may indicate a better rating, or a lower score may indicate a better rating—which system is being used must be clearly stated. Examples:

Rate a particular record from 1 to 10 with 10 being the best.
Rate a particular sports team from 1 to 20 with 1 being the best.
Rate the taste of a particular fast food item from 1 to 100 with 100 being the highest score.

Students can collect data using a rating system and then derive a **frequency distribution, an histogram** and compute a **mean.**

Scatter Plot: Sometimes data are collected in pairs. For instance (height, weight), (age, rating of TV show) or (shoe size, number of telephones in the home). These pairs of data can be graphed (see figure 4). Point A represents someone who is 60 inches tall and 120 pounds. B is 67 inches tall and weighs 150 pounds. **Eyeball fit** or **median fit line** can be used to construct a line that represents the data points on the scatter plot. The scatter plot can be analyzed qualitatively.

Are the points moving up or down as we go to the right? Is there a pattern of points or simply a "blob" of points?

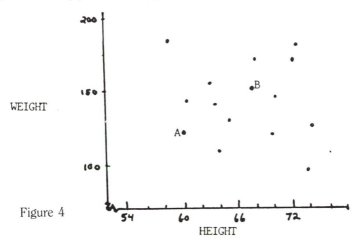

Figure 4

Stem and Leaf Plot: The stem and leaf plot combines the **frequency distribution** with the **histogram.** Instead of a bar graph, this graph uses a string of numbers representing the data. Given the data 16, 18, 19, 20, 23, 24, 24, 27, 28, 28, 31, 34, 37, 42, 48, the stem and leaf plot is shown in figure 5. The digits to the left of the vertical line are the ten's place digits. The assorted one's place digits show the distribution and amount of measurements for each ten's place digit. Note that there are two fours and two eights in the second line since there are two 24s and two 28s in the data. Back to back stem and leaf plots can be used to compare two sets of data (see figure 6).

1	6 8 9
2	0 3 4 4 7 8 8
3	1 4 7
4	2 8

Figure 5

9 5 3	1	6 8 9
8 7 3 1	2	0 3 4 4 7 8 8
7 6 0 0	3	1 4 7
5 5 3	4	2 8
0	5	

Figure 6

TEACHING MATHEMATICS

Murray Siegel teaches at Walton High School in Marietta, Georgia. For further information on his middle grades mathematics program, contact:

Murray H. Siegel, Ph.D.
Walton High School
1590 Bill Murdock Road
Marietta, GA 30062

STRATEGIES IN GEOMETRY FOR THE MIDDLE/JUNIOR HIGH SCHOOL

by Lawrence S. Menovich

Geometry is very different from the general mathematics taught in the middle/junior high school. We live in a world of geometry, yet we use only our classrooms to point out the concepts of points, lines, planes, parallels, and perpendiculars. The students look at what the teacher identifies and that's it. There is no spark of enthusiasm, no excitement, no life to what has been done. The textbooks tell us that "two points determine a unique straight line" as you pick up a pencil and hold it between your index fingers. Three points determine a plane: you point out that a camera rests on a tripod, which touches the floor at three points. The class clearly is not impressed and it's sink or swim time. At this point, I choose to swim. I have three sharpened pencils which I tell the class will serve as the legs of the tripod. Then I tell them that I will put the floor on the tripod. I hold the pencils spread apart in one hand and place a piece of cardboard on the points. There is some life. I move the pencils around, up and down, spread out further or closer together, each time keeping the piece of cardboard balanced. It doesn't take too long before they really begin to see what is happening. I then take a fourth pencil and demonstrate that the cardboard may balance, but that there is a strong likelihood that it may only rest on three pencils. This is something that is different, and in the words of one student several years ago, "It's a good different because you can't do this with numbers."

The applications of geometry virtually imprison us. Every building into which we step foot is a geometric cell, visualized by geometric drawings and constructed according to the physical forces of nature. A single bicycle spoke can be bent by a child, yet a 200-pound person can ride on that bicycle. Swimming pools have thin steel walls, yet they hold thousands of pounds of water. A two-inch piece of metal bent at the right place will hold a 50-pound mirror on a plaster wall. Everywhere you look, there is an application of geometry, yet these things are all taken for granted by today's students. Each and every one of us applies the concepts of geometry thousands of times in our lives, whether it be as simple as selecting the right size box for mailing a package or deciding on a set of furniture based on its size and eye appeal.

Historically, at least among my students, geometry has been the least liked part of the mathematics curriculum. Some feared it because the topic was always skipped over in the elementary grades (that has changed in recent years) and others because there weren't "answers" like you get in 4+5. Even today, a lot of my students don't trust geometry. They admit to its having too many things to learn—definitions and theorems—and no other place in the curriculum to use it. This last argument seems to have some merit, as many students have pointed out that it often is the last, or nearly the last, chapter in the book. Their argument follows that if it were important, then it would appear much sooner.

There is a wealth of geometry-related activities and topics that will enrich the curriculum and entertain the student. Many of these are in the numerous supplementary publications available to teachers, some of which are referenced at the end of this article. Other activities can be developed from things done in class or from questions asked by the students—pure serendipity. While the text basics should be presented, it is the extra items that spell the difference between enjoyment and boredom. I like to change the extras from year to year, adding some items one year while deleting others, not because they don't work, but to keep from doing the same things over and over again. I've also found that by doing different exercises, students can't pass them on to younger friends or relatives.

Geometry is something that I like to start as early in the year as possible, with some classes during the second week of school. While doing the obligatory whole number review with lower ability classes, an activity such as the following can be inserted as a class exercise:

> Trace a path from start so that you accumulate the number of points in the circle above the diagram. The rules to this activity are: 1) you must follow only the marked paths—the diagonal lines—as though you were bouncing a ball off a wall; 2) you may not retrace any path you've already been on; 3) upon entering a circle, count the number of points in that

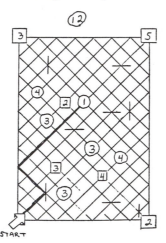

circle, and exit along any of the other paths; 4) you may enter any circle only once; and 5) once you enter a square, count the points and the game ends. Barriers in the interior of the diagram are to act as walls. The starting move has been entered into the diagram for you.

Clearly, this is an arithmetic puzzle, but the use of lines and angles is evident. Students are thinking geometry but not studying it yet. Additional exercise sheets can be produced easily by first designing the path, filling in the numbers and then by supplying the "dummy" numbers and barriers. Squares can be placed as you wish, but the three other corners must have squares.

The geometry that the middle/junior high student can successfully handle is indeed limited. That, however, should by no means limit what can be presented. With the very rarest of exceptions, a student of this age does not have the sophistication needed to apply more than one or two concepts at a time to a problem. My experience has been that the presentation of a theorem as a "theorem" turns kids off. It connotes a sort of stuffiness to the topic.

Most eighth graders couldn't "prove" the vertical angle theorem, but they could tell you that a certain pair of angles in a particular diagram have the same measure, especially if the diagram is blocked off, as shown, by using supplementary pairs of angles. This exercise shows that you can achieve a solution by looking at individual parts of a diagram in more than one way.

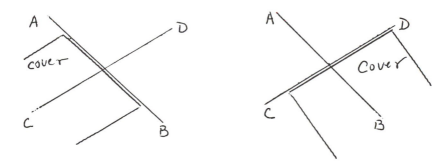

The concept of congruence, particularly with respect to triangles, and the writing of congruence statements is a part of most texts, and I've found that all of my students can master this concept. Congruence to this extent, though, is a one-day lesson. Do it—forget it. For the more able students, follow-up is a must, and I use the triangle congruence theorems to accomplish the goal. I do not teach the theorems per se, but I do get them introduced, and used.

A two-page lesson on symmetry does not have to end with one class and an assignment that night. Symmetry, both line and point, involves the concepts of reflection and rotation. One exercise set may involve finding the point or line of symmetry, while another will require that the student complete a drawing about a point or line of symmetry. Classroom follow-up provides an attempt at proving the drawing to be correct. (Use discretion here—some classes may not be able to handle this and will lose interest rapidly.) Line symmetry can be done easily by using scissors and folding, or by use of the MIRA, a plastic manipulative that produces images of a diagram "behind" its viewing surface. When viewed from the top, the MIRA looks like the letter "I"; MIRA is available through Creative Publications in Palo Alto, California. Point symmetry is proven by presentation and experimentation with the following statement: Points of a figure directly opposite each other with respect to the point of symmetry are the same distance from the point of symmetry. Referring to the following diagram, the line segments AA', BB', and CC' all pass through the point of symmetry, P.

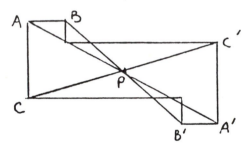

By using a compass, it can be shown that the segments AP and A'P, BP and B'P, and CP and C'P are congruent, and in combination with the vertical angle concept, pairs of congruent triangles, such as ABP and A'B'P are formed (note the Side-Angle-Side Theorem). Once this informal proof is completed, students can then readily complete drawings with point symmetry by creating their own pairs of congruent triangles.

Symmetry can lead into some interesting exploratory assignments. Go through the alphabet and identify those letters which have line symmetry, point symmetry, both, or none. Distribute square dot paper and have the class design, or redesign, the alphabet so that each letter has some symmetry—establish no other restrictions. Follow this by having them do the same on triangular dot paper. These activities require only a minimal amount of class time for explanation, allowing you to continue on with other work.

Every year since I have started doing symmetry, students have come by before or after classes to tell me of things they have seen in other classes, or outside the building, that have lines of symmetry clearly visible to them. They readily agree that for once geometry really does exist outside of a mathematics class.

Having given out dot paper, I invariably notice that some students will use the opportunity to play the game of dots. I will allow this only if they play by my rules. The concept of the game remains unchanged except that each pair of segments drawn must be symmetric about the center point of the square. No matter which player draws the even line segment, it must be symmetric, or the person loses his turn.

Another symmetry-based exercise is to complete a drawing like the one below so that the finished product contains shaded squares that are symmetric about both horizontal and vertical axes.

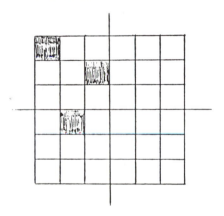

Symmetry and the MIRA can be used to discover many other facts. Recall the theorem that the altitude drawn to the base of an isosceles triangle is the perpendicular bisector of the base. This can be discovered by finding the line of symmetry of an isosceles triangle and responding to some careful questions on the teacher's part. List the students' observations on the chalkboard and lead the class into the appropriate discoveries. Similar activities can lead to many other discoveries, especially concerning the "special quadrilaterals." A question for further exploration: find polygons that have a one-to-one correspondence between lines of symmetry and number of sides.

Proving congruence of triangles in a Euclidean geometry class is often a very difficult thing for some students to handle because they can't see the congruence. Having already presented the use of congruent triangles in doing point symmetry drawings, I like to follow with explorations using the MIRA and reflections over any arbitrary axis line that is drawn. By tracing the image of a simple polygon, the students discover that congruence is preserved while the orientation of the figure is reversed. Further work is done by reflecting figures about axis systems at 90 degree angles, parallel axes, and axes that intersect the figure. At all stages of the work, students are required to compare the orientation of the reflection with the original. My concluding exercise is to present the class with the figure and its reflection and have them find the number and location of the axes.

Enrichment activities involving compass construction usually involve circle diagrams. Add something like construction of the Pepsi-Cola circle. Other activities include the Olympic 5-ring logo (not as easy as it looks) and designs based on squares. I have also added to this by assigning the construction of the alphabet, with the requirement that all letters must be based upon the constructions presented in class. Yet another activity, especially nice if it is a rainy day, is free art work, just so long as the work is generated by compass. Add some crayons and a reminder of symmetry, and you get some nice pieces for a bulletin board display.

The basic facts about points, lines, planes, angles, and triangles never seem to evoke much of a spark from students. Neither does a lesson on angle sums in polygons. Despite their reactions to your presentations, impress upon the students that these hold true for all figures drawn on the plane. It would be nice to get a question here, but after 15 years, I don't hold my breath anymore. Casually mention that there also exists a triangle with an angle sum of 270 degrees, and that the shortest distance between two points is not a line segment. This has never failed to work. Even the most disinterested students will perk up at those words. Pause for several minutes and watch the pencils trying to draw figures. While that is going on, I take a tennis ball out of my desk and start bouncing it on the floor. Not one student in any class has yet to see the connection between the ball and my statements prior to my demonstrating the solutions, but I will never forget the remark made by one youngster when I had finished talking about the geometry of the sphere: "Geometry isn't a flat topic after all."

Another discussion and exploration activity involves stable figures. Is a polygon with 5 sides more solid than one with 3 or 4 sides? Many students believe that more is better. Let them experiment with rulers and tape in groups of two or three. Have them construct the outlines of various polygons and tape their "vertices" together, then stand the figures up and determine which ones would be suitable for use in construction. Even though rulers and tape are flimsy, they should discover that the triangle is the least wobbly of all figures. I also point out that the diagonal brace in a fence-gate makes two triangles, and that virtually all major bridges incorporate the triangle into their superstructures. While they are busy, prepare to show them pictures of the geosphere at EPCOT and the Gateway Arch in St. Louis.

Discovering area formulas using geoboards requires a minimal amount of arithmetic at first. The concept of a unit of area is presented first by showing it to be a square formed by 4 adjacent nails.

As the number of nails on the boundary of a figure are increased, and as unused nails appear in the interior, the number of square units within the figure increases, or decreases, as the figures change. By charting the number of nails on the boundary (b) and in the interior (i), Pick's formula can be developed: $A=1/2b+i-1$.

Use your geoboard to have students determine rectangles and squares that cover a specific number of square units. Record the results on the board for reference and work on figures of different areas. After a while, ask if anyone notices a pattern developing. The class will have developed its own formula for finding the area of a rectangle. From here, move the rectangle at the top and change it to a parallelogram. The formulas for triangles and trapezoids can be developed from the parallelogram. Even if you find yourself presenting more than the class is deriving, the evolution of the formulas are still taking place before their eyes. This is far more valuable than merely writing them on the board and drawing diagrams to show bases and heights.

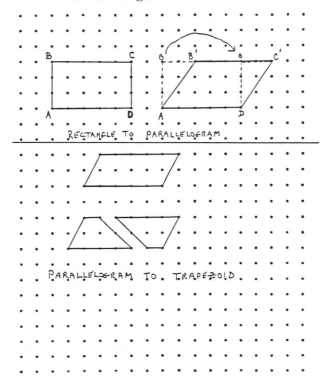

93

After lessons on squares and square roots of numbers have been completed, the geoboard can again become a valuable tool for exploration. Activities to include are: finding the number of different polygons with a maximum area; finding the polygon with the maximum number of sides; finding the polygon with the maximum perimeter.

Besides all of the foregoing suggested activities, I would like also to advocate the establishment of a long-term, multiphase project to be worked on at various times throughout the year. For 1984-85, I have presented a four-part unit consisting of network exercises, the four-color theory, spirolaterals, and tessellations. Three of the sections have been completed, and the tessellation segment is being worked on as this article is being written.

Such projects can challenge students to think geometrically. For example, the network phase began by presenting the classic Koenigsburg Bridge problem, which the class grudgingly admitted couldn't be solved. One student asked why they didn't build another bridge. We built another bridge, and tested the problem. One student didn't like where the new bridge was placed, so we moved it. We continued to put our new bridge in different positions, constantly trying to determine the solvability of our diagram. The class designed and tested other schematic drawings until we finally determined what a network had to have for it to be traversable.

Conclusion

I always have been interested in geometry, but in my early years in teaching, my students did not seem to share my enthusiasm. Thus, it was incumbent on me to instill some interest, to make geometry become something that students would come to enjoy. As mentioned earlier, the texts have limited presentations, thus the first obstacle was to find places where the topics could be presented. The second, and biggest obstacle was to find things to do that did not require vast amounts of prerequisite knowledge. This is still an ongoing venture, but I am well on the way.

In conclusion, I should note that not all of the activities mentioned are done with the same class. I am presently teaching four sixth, seventh, and eighth grade classes, and these activities are distributed among those classes. There are many other topics which can be readily revised and adapted to the study of geometry. Among these are polyominoes, topology, tangrams, curve stitching, and loci. All of these can be effectively presented to any level middle/junior high class, if the teacher takes an open-ended approach, so that explorations can be conducted either in class or as project assignments.

Lawrence S. Menovich is a mathematics teacher at East Middle School in Braintree, Massachusetts. For further information on his middle school geometry program, contact:

Lawrence S. Menovich
East Middle School
305 River Street
Braintree, MA 02184

REFERENCES

Bezuszka, Stanley, Margaret Kenny, and Linda Silvey. 1977. **Tessellations: The Geometry of Patterns.** Creative Publications. Palo Alto, CA.

Cech, Joseph P. and Joseph B. Tate. 1971. **Geoboard Activity Sheets.** Ideal School Supply. Oak Lawn, IL.

Del Grande, John. 1977. **Geoboards and Motion Geometry for Elementary Teachers.** Scott Foresman and Co. Glenview, IL.

Greenes, Carole, John Gregory and Dale Seymour. 1977. **Successful Problem Solving Techniques,** Creative Publications. Palo Alto, CA.

Krulik, Stephen and Jesse A. Rudnick. 1980. **Problem Solving—A Handbook for Teachers.** Allyn and Bacon. Boston, MA.

Maletsky, Evan, ed. September 1984. **Networks;** September 1983. **Spirolaterals.** National Council of Teachers of Mathematics: Student Math Notes. Reston, VA.

MIRA Math Co. 1973. **MIRA Math for Elementary School.** Creative Publications. Palo Alto, CA.

MIRA Math Co. 1973. **MIRA Activities for Junior High School Geometry.** Creative Publications. Palo Alto, CA.

Miller, William A. 1975. **Geometry Laboratory Activities I.** J. Weston Walch. Portland, ME.

Sobel, Max A. and Evan Maletsky. 1975 **Teaching Mathematics: A Sourcebook of Aids, Activities, and Strategies.** Prentice Hall, Inc. Englewood Cliffs, NJ.

TEACHING REMEDIAL MATHEMATICS: BREAKING THE VICIOUS CYCLE

by Carolyn Reese-Dukes

It is my contention that the amount of learning that takes place in a classroom of remedial mathematics students is more dependent upon affective factors than upon the particular mathematical materials and techniques used. My experience with remedial mathematical classes at various educational levels has convinced me that these students want to learn, and are capable of learning, mathematics—even those at the lowest level of achievement, those who **seem** least concerned, and those who are most rebellious. However, they seem to be caught in a vicious circle. They have a poor self-image—at least in regard to their ability to learn mathematics. Because they have no confidence in their ability to learn, they lack the degree of persistence and determination necessary to be successful. When they are once again unsuccessful, their belief that they cannot learn is reinforced, and the cycle begins all over again, becoming more and more debilitating with each experience (see figure 1).

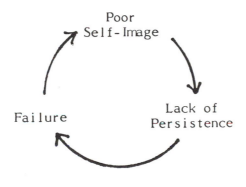

Figure 1

The teacher's primary task then is to intervene so as to break a link in this cycle, i.e., provide experiences that change self-image, thereby increasing success rate, and/or provide experiences that increase success rate, thereby improving self-concept. Much has been written about the importance of a positive self-concept and the experience of success to the learning of mathematics (National Council of Teachers of Mathematics, 1972; Creative Publications Inc., 1978). Therefore, it is not my purpose to argue for, or to substantiate, their importance. The purpose of this article is to present a series of specific techniques which have proven to be effective in significantly raising the achievement level of students in remedial mathematics classes. (Few, if any, of these ideas originated with me, but I have long since lost their sources.)

Improving the Student's Self-Image

The first task in improving self-image is to demonstrate caring and respect to each student as an individual. In order to communicate respect, the teacher must **genuinely care** about students and how much they learn. There can be no substitute for this, and it cannot be faked. Assuming this caring exists, how can it be communicated to the student?

1. **Treat students as individuals.** At the beginning of each class, try to speak to each student **by name.** Occasionally converse with them about personal things.

2. **Allow students to express their feelings.** During the first class, discuss how and why the students were assigned to the class; tell them if they don't know. Ask how they feel about being in the class. Some will be angry; allow them to express their feelings. Conclude the class by expressing the belief that all of them can learn mathematics if it is taught appropriately. Tell them that the class will probably be different from their previous math classes, and that everyone of them **will learn** some math and **will enjoy** it at least part of the time.

3. **Commence with and maintain high expectations.** Communicate this expectation subtly; do not make a big deal out of it. If students do not do their work when instructed, assume there is a problem in understanding and offer to help. Do NOT assume the student doesn't want to work and begin by chastising and/or lecturing.

4. **Involve the larger family unit.** Send home reports, or call parents, to make **positive** statements about the students. Include such things as getting to the class on time, finishing some work each day, being respectful and pleasant to others, obeying rules, etc. Avoid communicating with parents **only** when you need their help in resolving a problem. Make sure that the first communication is a positive one.

5. **Allow students to work together.** Encourage students to help other students and to seek help from others. Provide opportunities for group work, and establish groups so that there is a wide range of knowledge and ability.

6. **Give positive feedback.** Include some positive statement in every interaction with students. This is not to say that there should be no negative statements, but that they should be presented along with at least one positive statement. For example, when students are found cheating (or attempting

to), I begin by saying that I'm pleased that they care so much about the grade they receive, and then point out the problems involved with this behavior.

7. **Refuse to accept negative self-statements.** When students make a negative statement about their ability, help them change to a neutral statement. For example, when a student says, "I can't do this," I suggest he or she change the statement to, "I don't know how to do this; will you help me?" If the student says, "I'm dumb in math," perhaps this student will be willing to change it to, "I have trouble with math." While these are subtle differences, one communicates despair, the other indicates hope.

Ensuring Successful Mathematical Experiences

1. **Ensure that instruction is at a level where every student can experience quick success.** This may be done by assessing each student's current knowledge and individualizing the instruction accordingly. (It should be pointed out, however, that individualization alone will not ensure success.) There must be plenty of teacher-student interaction and adequate record-keeping to ensure up-to-date knowledge of each student's progress.

In cases where individualization does not seem feasible, make sure the first assignment given the class is one that **everyone** can do. Be careful, however, that it is not so elementary that it is humiliating and/or boring. The level of the task can be elevated by allowing the use of calculators, multiplication tables or other calculating aids, or it can be a task for which there is no right or wrong answer.

When instruction is not individualized there must be at least different levels of assignments, with students being able to choose the level. The minimum level of assignment should be within the grasp of every student, and the most challenging assignment must be difficult enough to keep all students active.

2. **De-emphasize memorization of basic facts.** While it is, of course, important that students learn basic facts, many students' view of themselves as "stupid in math" is based upon the fact that they don't know their multiplication tables. However, I have found that many of the brighter students—those who can solve two-step word problems with ease—do not know basic facts. It is not a sign of mathematical ability, and students should not be denied the opportunity to learn more difficult and exciting things while they also focus on memorization of facts.

When the task is primarily calculation, make sure students know how to derive answers and point out to them that they can find the correct answer. Observe their process of deriving the answer, and give suggestions for speeding up the process. Build up speed in recall by giving drill in enjoyable, nonthreatening ways. Be careful, however, not to have students engage in activities which might embarrass them in front of the class. Do not tie grades too strongly to knowledge of basic facts. Point out how knowledge of the basic facts will speed up their work and make it less frustrating or boring.

Allow students to see that mathematics consists of more than calculation by including other content such as problem solving and geometry in the curriculum. Also, allow them the opportunity to learn how to solve practical problems associated with working, buying, banking, traveling, and home improvements, for example, by allowing the use of calculators for the more difficult calculations. It is important to remember that while knowledge of basic facts is often very helpful, it is not essential to survival—except, perhaps, in school! I have a constant reminder of this in my own home. My husband is a professor of psychology and handles statistical work quite well in his research; he does not know what 9×7 is, without computing it!

3. **Do not allow students to practice errors.** Somewhere students have acquired the idea that any work is better than nothing; however, totally incorrect work reinforces their sense of failure. Encourage them to ask for assistance when they are unsure about what they are doing, and have an established procedure for doing this. Provide enjoyable activities from which they can choose, while they are waiting for assistance. Such activities can be found in **Aftermath** (Creative Publications 1975).

   When students make errors, take time to **diagnose the problem.** Students often erase their work when they find the answer is incorrect. Insist that they leave it, and ask them to explain what has been done. They have difficulty with this, but it aids concentration and often results in their finding their own error—another confidence builder. If a conceptual error is noted, point out the error and explain how to correct it. Observe the student's work until understanding is demonstrated.

4. **Give positive feedback for ANY correct work, rather than reserving it for correctness of the final answer.** If a student writes down the problem, you may say, "That's good, you've gotten started." As each step is completed (even if you are prompting), praise the work. When correcting work, point out what steps are correct, rather than those that are incorrect. (Don't use red ink; many students associate it with failure.)

5. **When you are sure students know how to proceed, firmly demand that some work be produced every day.** When students are not working (even misbehaving), begin by assuming it is because they do not know how to proceed. It may be that they could proceed but are afraid of failure. Quietly go to the student and ask if you can help. If the student says that help is not needed, state that you are pleased about that and ask to see what has been done. Praise what has been done and provide any instruction that seems needed. If the student acknowledges the need for help, ask to see what has already been done (even if it was done the day before), point out that the student has been successful, and then proceed with assistance. If possible, remain with the student until at least one problem has been done correctly. If you leave before understanding has been demonstrated, you may have left the student worse off than before—with a stronger sense of inadequacy for not being able to do the work with the teacher's help. If you are wondering how you can possibly give one student this much time, the work probably needs to be divided into smaller tasks. For example, the task may be to decide where the first number in the quotient is to be placed, rather than finding the quotient. When the student has done ten of these problems successfully, there follows a sense of accomplishment that might have occurred if the first task had been to solve the division problem.

6. **Ensure that students who work and progress will receive at least a C.** Remember, grades are important to **all** students. Tie the grade to the amount of work that is successfully completed. Help students to set goals and to monitor their progress toward the goal. You may have students sign performance contracts, stating how many units they intend to complete and showing what grade will be received for that amount of work. Provide an opportunity for **frequent** comparisons of the amount of work completed and the agreed-upon goal. Charts or graphs may be used for this purpose, but they may be displayed **only** if the student chooses.

7. **Reward students (other than with grades) who show exceptional progress.** Have more than one criteria for "exceptional" work. I use a "Superstars" bulletin board, which lists the names of students who completed the most units, who are working at the highest level, or who had 100% test averages. (Those students who complete the fewest units have the best chance of getting 100% test averages, since they take fewer tests.) I have also awarded certificates, cards of congratulations, and pencils which have "Math Superstar" printed on them.

8. **Help students perceive their successes.** Have students keep all their work in a notebook or folder. At the end of the grading period, they can see how

much work they have done. I keep all their work until the end of the year, when they can see how much work was done all together. At both the beginning and end of the year, I ask the students to write down (or check off) what math they already know how to do. They compare these lists to see how much they have learned. It also provides opportunities to compare pre- and post-test scores.

Conclusion

The techniques presented here are only some of the ways teachers of remedial mathematics classes can intervene to break the vicious cycle in which so many students are caught. Conscious attention must be given to interacting with students in such a way as to enhance their self-image and to provide them with experiences which will ensure mathematical successes. Though the cycle is vicious, it can be transformed from a cycle of despair and failure to a cycle of hope and success. Perhaps one of my students said it better than I when she wrote, "The most important thing I've learned about math this year is I can do it."

Carolyn Reese-Dukes is the Chapter I mathematics teacher at Highland Heights Middle School in Nashville, Tennessee. For further information on her remedial program, contact:

Carolyn Reese-Dukes, MA, MSW
4860 Torbay Drive
Nashville, TN 37211

REFERENCES

Blaeuer, David A. 1980. "Values Clarification in the Mathematics Classroom." In **Resource Manual for Counselors/Math Instructors,** pp. 80-86. Washington, D.C.: The Institute for the Study of Anxiety in Learning.

Aftermath (I and II). 1975. Palo Alto, California: Creative Publications, Inc.

Didactics and Mathematics: The Art and Science of Learning and Teaching Mathematics. 1978. Palo Alto, California: Creative Publications, Inc.

National Council of Teachers of Mathematics. 1972. **The Slow Learner in Mathematics: Thirty-fifth Yearbook.** Reston, Virginia: National Council of Teachers of Mathematics.

DIAGRAM DRAWING IN THE MATH CLASSROOM: EDDIE'S STORY

by Martin A. Simon

Eddie came into my classroom in September as a seventh grader, taller and physically more mature than the other students. His large frame and red hair made him clearly visible. My class was a combination seventh/eighth grade class of thirty students who spent five of seven periods a day with me. Eddie was a polite youngster, though at times his frustration led to violent outbursts.

As I got to know Eddie better, I learned that he had a history of poor academics which included his repeating the fourth grade. He cared about his academic performance and suffered still from being a year behind his original classmates. Two aspects of Eddie's performance caught my attention that year: one was his performance in math class and the other was his performance on imagery tasks.

Eddie was placed in the second of three groups (ability groupings) in math class. He was clearly at the lower end of that group at the outset. The year began with a review of whole number operations.

My instructional emphasis was on understanding the four basic operations (addition, subtraction, multiplication, and division) and being able to choose the appropriate operations in multistep word problems. This work led into a rigorous study of fractions again with emphasis on understanding and application in word problems.

We worked on the concepts of whole numbers and fractions with concrete manipulatives (tiles, fraction pies, geoboards) and explored them further with diagrams (see figure 1). The students developed new concepts through manipulation of these materials and diagrams in a problem solving context. I encouraged them to **discover** concepts and avoided **telling** them the concepts to be learned.

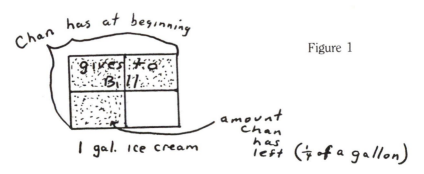

Figure 1

Eddie thrived in math class. He was achieving success for the first time in his life. His diagram solutions were creative, effective, and he was able to explain them fully. The other students, who had teased Eddie in past years, were now seeking his help with their math problems. He became my unofficial aide in his math group. During the winter, Eddie made a successful transition to the advanced math group.

Besides his dramatic improvement in math class, Eddie's performance on mental imagery tasks was also striking. During October and November, I was experimenting with the relation of visual imagery to spelling ability. While my findings on teaching spelling were inconclusive, I learned something valuable about Eddie in the process. Eddie had the most incredible imagery ability I had ever encountered. After I had led a guided imagery, Eddie would astound us all with the color, detail, and uniqueness of what he had "seen" in his mind. His narration of his images allowed us all to "see" them.

Later in the year, we used imagery and drawing to generate short stories and poems in English class. Once again, Eddie achieved at, what was for him, a new level of success. He wrote interesting, colorful stories of which he was proud and on which he worked hard to improve from one draft to another. During parent conferences, Eddie's mom, an aide in the school library, told me, "You seem to understand Eddie in a way that no one else has." She could not be more specific, but she had a strong feeling that somehow Eddie's needs were being met for the first time.

Discussion: In reflecting here on Eddie's academic turnaround, I wish to focus on the change in Eddie's performance in mathematics. We teachers know that a student who is consistently unsuccessful in mathematics throughout elementary school is almost certainly going to have difficulty in junior high and high school. This student is likely to wind up in a lower level math track and take no more mathematics than is required. As a result, math-related careers become unattainable and going to college may seem inappropriate.

Eddie's turnaround in math, therefore, was unusual. What can be learned from Eddie's case? What aspects of our math program might have contributed to Eddie's success? In answering the latter question, I focus on our use of concrete manipulatives and diagrams. This approach was motivated by my belief that conceptual learning progresses from concrete levels to more abstract levels. Two significant obstacles to math success seem to be overcome by such an approach. The overcoming of these two obstacles may explain the dramatic change in Eddie's performance.

The first obstacle has to do with the nature of mathematics learning. The concepts learned in mathematics tend to be hierarchical; that is, more advanced concepts are built on previously learned concepts. Thus, the failure to learn early concepts can frustrate attempts to learn more advanced material. As an example, consider the student work shown in figure 2. The solution shown for this fraction problem is one that, as a middle school teacher, I've seen repeatedly. It is usually not a "careless" mistake. It is made by students who have never understood the principle of regrouping which was taught in the primary grades. Thus, we as upper-grade teachers are faced with a dilemma. Do we as teachers go back to the source of the problem if the problem developed several years before?

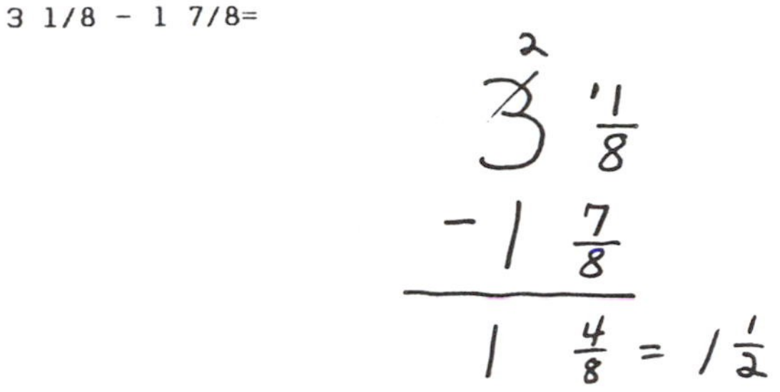

3 1/8 - 1 7/8=

$$3\,\overset{2}{}\,{}^{1}\!\tfrac{1}{8}$$
$$-\,1\,\tfrac{7}{8}$$
$$\overline{1\,\tfrac{4}{8}\,=\,1\tfrac{1}{2}}$$

Figure 2

The failure of students to learn a concept, such as regrouping, which has been taught to them several times, is often a result of insufficient **concrete** experience on which to build an understanding of the concept. The student who solved the problem in figure 2 has no concrete (physical) or mental model of regrouping. Instead the student attempts to recall from memory the correct procedure, a procedure which is not connected, for him or her, to the physical world. I make two assumptions here. One, the student's progress will be blocked by not understanding a basic concept such as regrouping. Two, giving the student (once again) an explanation and demonstration (teaching as **telling**) of how to do such a problem is not likely to be successful.

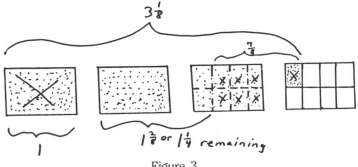

Figure 3

Continuum from concrete to abstract

Figure 4

The diagram solution that Eddie might have used (see figure 3) allows an exploration of the problem at a level that is more concrete (see figure 4) than the symbols used in figure two. The use of diagrams can supply the needed foundation on which to build an abstract understanding of regrouping in subtraction of fractions. The subsequent use of the subtraction algorithm for fractions can then be based on understanding.

The second obstacle to Eddie's achievement in math was an apparent mismatch between Eddie's predominant mode of learning and thinking and the process by which math is commonly taught. Work on brain hemisphere specialization (Hunter 1976, Brandwein and Ornstein 1977, Wheatly 1978), while inconclusive and somewhat speculative, has given us a useful metaphor for looking at two distinct modes of thought and learning. For example, Eddie's tremendous talent for visual imagery, coupled with his previous lack of academic success, suggest that his strengths may lie in the right hemisphere. In particular, those strengths include seeing the whole pattern rather than sequentially analyzing the parts, and working from a visual image rather than an ordered set of ideas. The picture drawing gave Eddie a chance to see the relationships in the problem which resulted in an understanding and an increased confidence with the work.

It is important to note that although picture drawing seems particularly adaptive to "right-brain" students such as Eddie, one of the aims of classroom teaching should be the development of "right-brain" and "left-brain" skills in all students. Traditionally we have undervalued and undertaught skills involving imagery, whole pattern recognition, and intuition. In doing so, we have shortchanged all learners.

Conclusions: Students like Eddie are failing to achieve competence and confidence in math because they have failed to understand fundamental concepts (early on) due to a lack of concrete experience, and because the commonly used symbol manipulative approach to math instruction fails to harness their talents and successful learning modes. Diagram drawing can be one factor in correcting this situation.

Unfortunately, however, math teachers, particularly those who teach above the elementary grades, tend to avoid the use of diagrams. From working with other teachers I conclude that there are three main reasons why teachers do not use diagrams and concrete materials:

1. Teachers face tremendous pressure to cover a large number of different topics. Lecture/demonstration takes less time than exploration with concrete materials and diagrams.

2. The teachers themselves have not learned math using concrete materials and diagrams. As a result, many do not think pictorially and are not comfortable teaching with diagrams.

3. Initial attempts to use concrete materials and diagrams have met with resistance from students who consider such work to be only for younger students and who are comfortable with the regular way of instruction.

If these obstacles are to be eliminated, and valuable tools like diagrams and concrete materials are to be used, the following recommendations must be followed.

1. School districts must recognize the difference between **covering** curriculum and **learning.** Teachers are commonly required to cover more than one new concept for every period of instruction. As a result, effective and essential techniques such as exploration with manipulatives and diagrams and monitoring learning for the purpose of reteaching unlearned concepts, are considered too time-consuming. Some of the curriculum pressure must be removed from teachers to allow them to focus on student learning rather than the number of topics covered. I was fortunate, when Eddie was my student, to be working under an administrator who was supportive of my work. He understood that rigorous teaching for understanding takes time, thus necessitating the omission of some of the topics in the textbook.

2. Teachers must take the time, themselves, to work through problems with diagrams in order to become familiar with this tool and become more aware of its power. I have been working with diagrams intensively for eight years and I continue to learn more about the use of diagrams to solve problems and to develop concepts.

3. Students must be helped to learn the value of this tool. Eddie's class was no less resistant initially to this work than any other class. I helped them to understand some of the theory on which the diagram approach is based (e.g., that learning progresses from the concrete to the abstract), and I showed

them diagram solutions to problems which seemed beyond their abilities. Slowly they began to see diagrams and concrete materials as empowering and something to fall back on when they ran into difficulties.

Diagram drawing proved to be equally valuable for the advanced students. One of my more rewarding moments came after we had worked rigorously with fraction pictures for several months, developing each concept before learning algorithms for symbol manipulation. I had given the following problem to see if my students would have the insight to work backwards.

Elise brought home her paycheck. 1/3 of it went to rent. 1/4 of what remained went for food. 5/6 of the money that was then left went to pay the other bills, leaving her with $100. What was the amount of her paycheck?

I had **not** thought to try a diagram solution for this problem. Cindy raised her hand, "Mr. Simon, I just drew a picture." Cindy went up to the chalkboard and showed us the following simple, elegant solution.

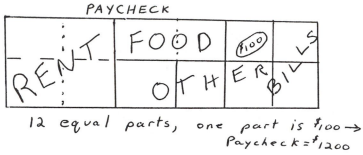

Figure 5

Diagram is only one tool for improving math instruction. However, if it allows even a few of our Eddies and Cindys to turn math failure into math success, isn't it worth exploring? My experience is that other students benefit, too. Diagram drawing helps students in general to increase their conceptual understanding and develop a powerful "heuristic" strategy (Polya 1945) for problem solving.

Martin A. Simon is the Director of SummerMath for Teachers at Mt. Holyoke College. He has taught sixth to tenth grades in Penn Valley and Berkeley, California. For further information on his mathematics program, contact:

Martin A. Simon
SummerMath for Teachers
Mt. Holyoke College
South Hadley, MA 01075

REFERENCES

Brandwein, P. and R. Ornstein. 1977. Duality of the mind. **Instructor.** 86:56-58.

Edwards, B. 1979. **Drawing on the Right Side of the Brain,** p. 40. Los Angeles: J.P. Tarcher, Inc.

Hunter, M. 1976. Right-brained Kids in Left-brained Schools. **Today's Education.** 65:45-48.

Polya, G. 1945. **How to Solve It,** Princeton: Princeton University Press.

Wheatly, G.H. 1978. Hemispheric Specialization and Cognitive Development: Implications for Mathematics Education. **Journal for Research in Mathematics Education.** 9:20-32.

MATH LAB:
TURNING STUDENTS AROUND

by Susette Jaquette

When Dana began her junior year of high school, she "hated math." She had failed her previous math course and could not understand why her counselor suggested taking yet another. Dana was enrolled in Math Lab.

James had begun his tenth grade year enrolled in a basic skills math course. By the end of the first nine weeks, it was evident that James would not pass the course. James was added to Math Lab.

Joyce was a bright, outgoing, athletic student enrolled in algebra, until a freak accident left her mentally and physically impaired. Joyce was enrolled in Math Lab.

Math Lab is a remedial high school math course designed to give students a positive, successful math experience. Students receive a combination of teacher-directed group instruction and computer-assisted individual instruction. Those enrolled in the course include students who failed or did poorly in their junior high basic math course, students recommended by junior or senior high school math teachers, and special education students. Non-English speaking students also may enroll. The class is especially well-suited to those students with holes in their overall math knowledge ("swiss-cheese" math skills), since they may also piggy-back Math Lab with a concurrent math course.

The present day Math Lab course evolved from a computer-assisted remedial math course that used six on-line computers with a drill and practice program supplemented with worksheets. When I inherited the course, we added group instruction time and switched to Apple IIe microcomputers for the computer-assisted instruction. The switch to microcomputers meant finding a new software package. Several drill and practice software packages were previewed. The Milliken **Math Sequences** package best fit our needs. The package contains twelve disks covering number readiness, addition, subtraction, multiplication, division, laws of arithmetic, integers, decimals, fractions, percent, measurement, and equations. An administrative package allows assignment of specific types of problems and keeps track of what students have completed.

My first Math Lab class included seven special education students, six basic skills students, and one student for whom English was a second language. During group instruction, students worked problems on paper or at the board; they also chased each other around the room, screamed obscenities, stuck pencils in interesting places, and constantly reminded me that they hated math. The first time they were on task for more than five minutes, I celebrated. Needless to say, individualizing group instruction for such a variety of skill levels has been on ongoing task.

Motivation and classroom management were not problems during the computer-assisted instruction. The students were very eager to work on the disks. However, the CAI was not without problems. Total chaos and confusion best describe the first week, as fourteen students constantly yelled, "Teacher, teacher, I need help!" Seeing that a migraine was in the future if something did not change, I began yelling, "I need help, too!" A very understanding department chairperson and a supportive principal responded to my problem. A senior computer-science student was quickly assigned to the class as an aide. The Math Lab aide has proven invaluable to the class in terms of assisting students, writing programs, preparing disks, and retrieving information.

During the next two years, the Math Lab course guide was constantly being evaluated and modified. Attending workshops, seminars, talking to other teachers, and trial and error have all led to the development of a success-oriented eighteen-week course guide (see appendix).

The group instruction time includes a variety of activities. Those activities are testing, mental calculations, programming in Basic or Logo, class instruction and discussion, problem solving, and working logic puzzles and completing worksheets.

During the first week of group instruction, I try to collect as much information about the students as possible. A teacher-made written pretest is administered and informal oral testing is conducted. Test results can be used to determine the topics where remediation is needed as well as boundaries for group instruction. A student's reaction to testing can also be informative. When a pretest was given to Paul, a rather large, learning disabled student, he pushed the test off his desk and shouted, "Get out of my face, I hate you." My response, "Paul, are you trying to get on my good side?" did not get him to take the test but it did make him cover his face to hide a smile. I learned Paul was not confident with his math skills, used inappropriate behavior to hide his lack of knowledge, and, of course, did not hate me at all. Paul was assigned work on the addition sequence, at a level that would ensure success.

Test results can also be used to ensure that a student has been properly placed. When Bill, a basic skills student began his pretest, he shouted, "This is baby s**t!" I diagnosed Bill was either misplaced, had swiss-cheese skills, or a vision problem. Upon reviewing Bill's test, I decided that he was in fact misplaced. The next day, Bill transferred to a basic skills class. Similarly, the information collected during the first week is used to assign each student a task that will lead to success.

Once the testing has been completed, students practice mental calculations in the four basic operations using whole numbers. Many of the "Mental Math" problems are taken from the work of Charles E. Allen, an instructional specialist and teacher in the Los Angeles Unified School District, Los Angeles, California. The following are a sample of mental math routines:

- Question and Answer: The teacher walks among the students, points to a student and states a problem, such as 6×7. The student has a designated number of seconds in which to answer. After that time, anyone may give the correct answer.

- I'm Thinking of a Number: The teacher says, "I'm thinking of a number that when you subtract 5 from it, you get 7. What's my number?" More than one operation can be used at a time.

- Join My Count: The teacher begins stating a sequence of numbers, such as 1, 6, 11, 16, 21... The students try to join in as soon as possible.

- Add the Numbers You Hear Me Say: The teacher tells a story which includes numbers. The students must find the sum of all the numbers.

- Columns and Rows of Random Digits: Using an overhead transparency or the chalkboard, students view several columns and rows of random digits. The teacher can ask students to perform operations on different rows and columns. The teacher may also perform an operation on a row or column and then read off the numbers. The students try to name the operation and the row or column.

Mental calculations are often very difficult for remedial students. Michelle, a highly motivated, learning disabled student refused to answer any mental calculation problems. Each time a question was directed to her, she would bow her head and say, "Don't ask me" or "I don't know." It finally occurred to me that she did not know how to calculate mentally. After I modeled my thought processes and selected some sure-fire success problems, Michelle began calculating mentally.

A popular group activity with the students is programming. Teaching programming skills is also popular with me since it can more readily be individualized for all students. At present, I teach programming using Basic, but would also like to include Logo in the future. For example, students learn to use the print statement.

```
10 PRINT "name"              40 PRINT "date"
20 PRINT "Math Lab"          50 END
30 PRINT "Huron High School"
```

Students are then asked to type their programs into the computer in the following order, lines 30, 50, 10, 40 and 20. After running the programs, students discuss why the output is ordered 10, 20, 30, 40, and 50. Upon completing this exercise, Ron, a special education student, exclaimed, "So that's why they're like that!" Ron confessed that he had always thought that you had to memorize numbers. When he realized that numbers were sequential, his perception of mathematics was completely transformed and his math skills improved greatly.

Other programming assignments may include writing a program that will a) add two numbers, b) multiply three numbers, c) divide a number in half, d) convert a mixed number to an improper fraction, e) solve a proportion, or f) change a decimal to a percent.

"Math Talk" activities involve instruction and discussions about numbers. The Math Talk session on integers includes the following:

- instruction on placing points on a number line,

- discussion about the similarities between a ruler and a number line,

- instruction on ordering positive integers,

- discussion on the similarities between a thermometer and a number line,

- instructions on ordering positive and negative integers.

Worksheets and enrichment activities that reinforce topics can also be introduced (see references).

Many students are reluctant to talk about math topics since their skills are so low. An abstract discussion of the similarities between a thermometer and a number line may not induce participation. However, asking in what part of the country a student would like to live and inquiring about the temperature of that region will produce a response. Carl, a special education student, asked me if this was "college work." He obviously recognized that we were talking about more than 80 degree weather in Florida, that we were talking about mathematics as it applies to the real world.

Problem solving and logic activities are basically puzzles that can be completed mentally or with calculators. Again, I have to stress that teachers' modeling of thought processes is a must for remedial students. For example, after passing out a maze puzzle to students, I use a transparency to show them how I would solve such a puzzle. Another example is the following activity that can help students to solve multiplication problems with greater confidence and speed.

ON BOARD

$$28 \atop \underline{\times\ \square} \atop 112$$

TEACHER: When I see a problem like this, I say to myself, the missing number multiplied by 8 must end in a 2. My mind then runs through the multiples of 8, $(8\times1=)8$, $(8\times2=)16$, $(8\times3=)24$, $(8\times4=)32$. Now I try 28×4 to see if it equals 112. It does and I am finished. This process may seem rather long but with practice you will become much quicker. Let's try one together this time.

ON BOARD

$$14 \atop \underline{\times\ \square} \atop 98$$

TEACHER: The missing number multiplied by
STUDENTS: 4
TEACHER: must end in an
STUDENTS: 8
TEACHER: The multiples of
STUDENTS: 4 are $(4\times1=)4$, $(4\times2=)8$.
TEACHER: $14\times2=28$, not 98. Continue

Of course, during this entire dialogue Johnny and Sally are exchanging glances, erasers, and cootie shots. So, you may have to repeat this exercise n-cubed times. Remember this is not a video. It is reality.

One day, I had given students three numbers (13, 25, 46) and two operations (+ and −) to arrange so the final answer would equal 8. Carl had worked for a few minutes and then asked to see the answer. I responded by saying that I would have to work it out on paper. He looked at me and said, "You mean you can't do all the problems in your head?" It had never occurred to Carl that I worked out many of the problems prior to class.

The group instruction activities described above are "high energy" activities for the teacher. This level of activity cannot be maintained throughout an entire semester unless, of course, this is the only class you teach all day (I have five, thank you). A "low [teacher] energy" activity is assigning self-correcting worksheets corresponding to the students' level. I refer to these as application problems since students are applying the skills they have learned to solving problems. Self-correcting worksheets also allow students to apply logic skills in trying to deduct if a problem set is correct.

The first week of computer-assisted instruction is devoted to familiarizing students with the hardware. Vocabulary, operational procedures, and rules are stressed. Each semester it seems I must expel one student for rough-housing around the equipment. It is a rule that cannot be compromised. It only took seeing a printer bounce off the floor one time to assure me that expulsion, not warning, was a consequence.

Bobby, the present Math Lab aide, wrote a program that enables the students to enter their class schedules and obtain a print-out. The step-by-step instructions guide students through hands-on experience. As students run other canned programs the first week, their fears are alleviated. When Ruth, a basic skills student, entered an incorrect answer, she would scream, "This thing hates me today. I'm not going to work." As Ruth gained a better understanding of the computer, she no longer thought it was plotting against her.

Students are given the task of recording their own progress on all computer-assisted work. A packet of worksheets is issued to each student. The packet contains a daily record form, self-correcting worksheets, and practice tests. The worksheets, along with a pencil or other supplies, can easily be kept in an interoffice envelope. Students pick up their envelopes upon entering the room and have everything they need to begin work.

Drill and practice assignments are entered on the appropriate disk for each student. Some students prefer to work on only one disk at a time; others prefer two or three. As long as the student is working, I am happy! When a student completes a disk, a short written test and short informal oral test are administered. Any question that a student has difficulty with can be reassigned, reviewed, and retested. Certain topics which are extremely difficult can also be enriched with worksheets.

Several times through the semester, students break from their drill and practice disks to play educational computer games (see references), which can be enjoyable and motivating. Students can shoot darts at balloons on a number line, answer a division problem correctly and shoot down an asteroid, race cars by correctly answering addition problems, solve logic puzzles and race the clock in answering subtraction problems.

Conclusion

There are many components of Math Lab that contribute to its success. The combination of teacher-directed instruction and computer-assisted instruction gives students plenty of variety. An administrator who is supportive and understanding keeps teacher morale high and mechanical problems low. A sense of humor and a ton of compassion open effective communication between student and teacher. Modeling every skill and assuming nothing allows teachers to bring students the instruction they need. Most important, however, is that teachers realize the importance in helping each student seek success. Carl, after mastering an arcade-like division game, asked, "Do you think I'm famous?" I replied, "Yes, Carl, you're famous to me."

Susette Jaquette teaches mathematics at Ann Arbor Huron High School. Her efforts were recognized in the NEREX Study of Exemplary Mathematics Programs as an exemplary approach for the lowest-level high school student. For further information on her math lab program, contact:

Susette Jaquette
Ann Arbor Huron High School
2727 Fuller Road
Ann Arbor, MI 48105

APPENDIX

COURSE GUIDE: MATH LAB

WEEK	GROUP INSTRUCTION	COMPUTER-ASSISTED INSTRUCTION
1	Testing	Introduction to Computers
2	Mental Math (+,−,×,/,laws)	Drill and Practice Software
3	Programming in Basic or Logo	Drill and Practice Software
4	Math Talk (integers)	Learning Games
5	Mental Math (integers)	Drill and Practice Software
6	Problem Solving and Logic	Drill and Practice Software
7	Application Problems (integers)	Drill and Practice Software
8	Testing and Programming in Basic or Logo	Learning Games or Problem Solving Software
9	Math Talk (fractions/decimals)	Drill and Practice Software
10	Mental Math (fractions)	Drill and Practice Software
11	Mental Math (decimals)	Drill and Practice Software
12	Problem Solving and Logic	Problem Solving Software
13	Application Problems (fractions/decimals)	Drill and Practice Software
14	Geometry	Drill and Practice Software
15	Math Talk (percent)	Drill and Practice Software
16	Mental Math (percent)	Learning Games
17	Application Problems (percent)	Drill and Practice Software (review)
18	Review and Testing	Drill and Practice Software (review)

REFERENCES

BOOKS
EA—Denotes materials that can be used for enriching a topic.
PSL—Denotes materials with problem solving and logic activities.
SC—Denotes materials that are self-correcting.

Black, H. and S. Black. 1984. **Building Thinking Skills,** Midwest Publications, California. (PSL)

Bureloff, M., C. Johnson and R. Roes. 1977. **Calculators, Number Patterns and Magic,** Activity Resources Company, Inc., California. (PSL)

Clack, A. and C. Leitch. 1975. **Mathamerica,** Midwest Publications Company, Inc., Michigan. (EA, SC)

Clack, A. and C. Leitch. 1973. **Math Amusements In Developing Skills,** Midwest Publications Company, Inc. (EA, SC)

Crouch, William A. 1969. **Coordinated Cross-Number Puzzles,** McCormick-Mathers Publishing Company, Inc., Ohio. (EA, SC)

Edwards, J., R. Edwards and D. Hestwood. 1977. **Fortified Fractions,** The Math Group, Inc., Minnesota. (EA, SC)

Eldenburg, Paul. 1977. **Picture Graphing,** The Math Group, Minnesota. (EA)

Hestwood, Diana. 1981. **Basic Skills Bonanza: Adding and Subtracting Fractions,** Gamco Industries, Inc., Texas. (EA, SC)

Holmberg, V., M. Laycock and D. Seymour. 1975. **Aftermath,** Creative Publications, California. (PSL)

Jacobs, Russell F. 1982. **Problem Solving With the Calculator,** Jacobs Publishing Co., Arizona. (PSL)

Marcy, S. and J. Marcy. 1973. **Mathimagination,** Creative Publications, Inc., California. (EA, SC)

Mathematics Basic Skills Development Project (Minneapolis Public Schools). 1977. **Beefing Up Basic Skills,** The Math Group, Inc., Minnesota. (EA, SC)

Miller, Don. 1979. **Calculator Explorations and Problems,** Cuisenaire Company of America, Inc., New York. (PSL)

Seymour, Dale. 1981. **Developing Skills In Estimation,** Dale Seymour Publications, California. (PSL)

Seymour, D. and R. Gidley. 1970. **Mathematics Enrichment: Eureka,** Creative Publications, Inc., California. (EA, PSL)

Smart, Margaret A. 1983. **Focus on Pre-Algebra,** Activity Resources Company, Inc., California. (EA)

Swienciki, Lawrence. 1974. **Adventures With Arithmetic,** Creative Publications, Inc., California. (EA, SC)

COMPUTER SOFTWARE

Basic Number Facts, 1982; **Fractions,** 1982. Control Data Publishing Company, Inc., San Diego, CA. Plato Educational Software.

Alien Addition, 1982; **Minus Mission,** 1982; **Meteor Multiplication,** 1982; **Demolition Division,** 1982. Developmental Learning Materials, Allen, TX.

Comp-u-solve, 1983. Educational Activities, Inc., Freeport, NY.

Decimals, 1980. Edu-Ware Services, Inc., Agoura, CA.

Math Sequences, 1980. Milliken Publishing Company, St. Louis, MO.

MATH LAB—FOR EVERYONE

by Bonnie Mellow

Introduction

Math lab is usually seen as a device for helping slower students to catch up. At our school, we have made it much more than that—a device for average students, as well as slower students, to explore cooperative problem solving, to learn how to use each other as learning resources, and to build spatial and logical skills. The program has proved especially successful with girls.

It's Monday morning: the eight-minute break between second and third period is two minutes old. A small group of Introductory to Algebra students cluster around our class chart taped to our closet door.

> Carrie: What do we have?
> Shannon: 6A. Which ones are computers?
> Carrie: I think its 8A and 8B. We have 8A in two weeks.

Each girl crossed out "6A" on the fourth square next to her name, then began searching the three-room complex for an orange tub with "6A" in large black contact paper on each end. Two girls from my colleague Kathy's Math Skills II class were sitting side-by-side in the four-desk math lab station when Carrie and Shannon arrived. An open box of multilink cubes sat next to the orange tub.

> Carrie: Hi, Beth. Do you and Tracy have "6A" too?

As the girls talked, Tracy snapped several cubes together in a strange shape. She rotated and rearranged her creation several times.

> Carrie: We better get started. Are these cubes all we need?

Shannon checked the "materials needed" list printed on the file folder inside the orange tub, "box of multilink cubes and graph paper for the extension," she answered.

Both sets of students took a packet from the file folder. Each lab partner signed her name on one of the double name spaces. Now the work and credit would belong to both.

Most of the 60 students were at one of 16 assigned stations when the bell rang. All four girls focused their attention on the first set of instructions: "There are exactly eight ways to put four cubes together. Build all eight solid shapes. . ."

121

TEACHING MATHEMATICS

Welcome to math lab.

As teachers, we are interested in new ideas or methods to use in class. The problem for many of us is not lack of ideas, however, but how to implement them. Few schools have classroom sets of games, geoboards, calculators or even enough glue and scissors for each student; now we have to deal with computers! There are great software packages on the market, but most schools can only afford to buy one or two copies of each. Our curriculum is often limited by time, energy, and materials. For my colleague, Kathy Pfaendler and me, the solution was to develop and implement a math lab program.

Each quarter, students rotate through eight different labs. Individual lab packets are designed to be completed by a team of two students within a class period. At each lab station, there are two pairs of lab partners. Each station is doubled. This allows math lab to serve two classes at one time. Each team uses separate equipment, but because of the packet organization, usually no more than two sets of any item is needed.

All materials needed to complete each lab are stored in numbered tubs (old clay storage tubs with new paint). The tubs are set out prior to class, thereby reducing organizational time. Students find their lab station by checking a class chart. Math lab is designed to serve up to 64 students, although 50 is ideal.

Ten minutes into period three. Beth's hand is in the air.

Beth: I think we found all eight shapes. It says you have to initial the packet.

Me: Close, but it looks like you only have seven. If you turn this one, these two are the same.

Tracy: Wait, here's one more.

Many girls have a hard time visualizing three-dimensional figures, manipulating materials and grasping spatial relationships; however, Tracy seems to be an exception.

When math lab started in 1978, programs were blossoming for handicapped, remedial, and gifted students. Unfortunately, little attention or funds were allocated to the remaining 80 percent of our student population. However, enrichment activities, problem solving, and cooperative learning are valuable skills for all kids. Although some "special" students are in lab sections, our goal was to give the average student something special. This is our target population. Math lab offers variety and discovery learning through using hands-on activities one day a week.

By the end of their eighth-grade year, most of our students will complete 64 lab packets including topics such as:
- logic and problem solving strategies
- metric and nonmetric geometry
- number patterns and sequences
- math art
- consumer items
- computer activities
- estimation and visualization
- probability and statistics

Math lab materials include everything from toothpicks to computers. Each teacher must assume responsibility for equipment maintenance, since no extra staff is allocated to operate the math lab.

Period three plus twenty minutes.

> Kevin: I don't get this.
> Me: What part don't you understand?
> Kevin: The whole thing.
> Me: What does your lab partner think?
> Kevin: Steve doesn't get it either.
> Me: How about the other team at this station?
> Kevin: They are still on another page.
> Me: Read it out loud.
> Kevin: Bisect each line segment. . .
> Steve: Oh, I get it! See, I did the last page and Kevin's s'posed to do this one.
> Me: But the introduction for this problem is on the last page. Talk it over and I'm sure that you will both understand.

Learning to work with another person can be hard, but the lab organization allows kids to learn together in an encouraging environment. Most students enjoy this opportunity and become more involved with mathematics than they would in a traditional setting. Because students work without teacher input, each packet is self-explanatory. Whenever appropriate, students are asked to look for patterns and generalize abstract ideas from concrete lab experiences.

For example, the girls in 6A are asked to build shapes that double each dimension of the four-cube solids, predict the number of cubes needed to double any solid, and test their prediction. Carrie and Tracy both have hands in the air.

Carrie:	We finished!
Me:	So I see. Was it hard?
Tracy:	Yes, at first. Then we made a bunch of these large cubes and all you have to do is move them around.
Shannon:	I need some extra credit. Let's do the extension, we have time.

Math lab packets are used by students from many ability groupings. Therefore, most labs have extensions that are required work and extra credit, depending upon the class. Because the lab is part of our mathematics program, packets are corrected and account for 20 percent of the class grade.

Period three ends in five minutes. Two student helpers turn off one bank of lights in each room. A few "shhh's" can be heard as silence fills the large open area.

| Kathy: | It's clean up time. You have four minutes. Raise your hand when you are ready to be checked. |

As we check each station, students move about discarding used paper or putting finished packets in assignment baskets. This is the only time that students may leave their lab stations. Six hundred people use the facility each week; therefore, vandalism is not tolerated. We have few discipline problems because every student knows that unacceptable behavior will suspend their lab privileges. All materials are checked before a class is dismissed.

Some people questioned the value of math lab during its first year, but that was before standardized test results showed that students participating in math lab scored equally well or better than nonlab students. Although the program was not developed for girls, they seem to benefit the most. This is noteworthy, because many young women graduate from high school without the adequate math, science, or computer preparation needed for more technical educational and occupational opportunities. Working women are concentrated in clerical, service, and social service jobs and earn about sixty percent of the wage earned by working men.

Math lab gives students and teachers a much needed break in textbook-style math. Limited planning time coupled with large class loads make it impossible to meet the individual needs of our students with traditional whole-class instruction. Our students have benefited from the varied learning opportunities, and my colleague Kathy and I have benefited from planning and working together.

The opportunities for Kathy and me to work together have been the extra payoff from math lab. Teachers need each other in ways that other professionals cannot imagine. The unique challenges we face like low public esteem, the pay scale, limited planning time, large class sizes, and negative press are best met with team efforts. By working in teams we can motivate and encourage each other. Our working conditions are best when we cooperate with each other, sharing the work and the joys of teaching.

Bonnie Mellow teaches mathematics and computers in grades seven, eight, and nine at the Mountain View Intermediate School in Beaverton, Oregon. For further information on her math lab, contact:

Bonnie Mellow
Mountain View Intermediate School
17500 Southwest Farmington Road
Beaverton, OR 97007

SPALT, INCORPORATED: AN APPLIED MATHEMATICS SIMULATION

by Sandra Spalt

Vocational-applied mathematics courses, as taught in many high schools, are a challenge to the classically trained mathematics teacher. One of the greater challenges is to make problems meaningful and to keep the students, who are not mathematically but vocationally oriented, interested and on task during April and May. These challenges were met at Red Bud High School by the formation of a company at the end of the third quarter grading period. The company, humbly called Spalt, Inc. is a simulation used as part of a one-year course offered to sophomores, juniors, and seniors in applied mathematics and has these goals:

1. To provide the student with the opportunity to do individual work with problems peculiar to the various vocations, i.e., welding, plumbing, nursing, food service, machining, carpentry, etc.

2. To provide the student with independent study experience, as well as career awareness.

3. To remedy the student's weaknesses in basic mathematics skills.

WE SOLVE PROBLEMS FOR TODAY AND TOMORROW! is our motto.

As employees of Spalt, Inc. all students are required to fill out a formal job application with references, fill out W-4 forms, keep a time card, check their wage statements (paychecks), and file for an income tax refund. These are managerial skills atop the requirements for continued employment which means working problems each day. Employees are required to choose three of twelve possible job units (carpentry, welding, nursing, clerical, machining, etc.) and to write a one-page report per unit on the job opportunities, requirements for entry, and salaries and rewards of that particular occupation. They then list their three top job choices in order of preference. Seniority is considered if more than four people request the same job assignment. Seniority is defined as seniors having preference over underclassmen! Depending upon class size, a foreman may be chosen on a weekly basis. The foreman is paid $1 per hour extra and is responsible for overseeing production (are they on task?) and cleanup (are files, books, and calculators put away?).

Students work independently or in groups, so my time is used to help with individual problems and to assign and grade tests. Students have individual contracts for their work units. These contracts are based upon their performance over the prior three quarters. If an individual in welding has trouble with adding and subtracting fractions but not with multiplying and dividing, then he or she is assigned all of the problems in welding on adding and subtracting but only every third one on multiplying and dividing. Assignments for the entire quarter are made in one negotiating session but are subject to review if the employee finds the work too redundant.

Students are paid $10 per hour (in bogus Spalt checks) for class work. Homework is reimbursed at the rate of $.25 per problem. Homework is given as overtime and may be requested by the student as extra work or used to compensate for wages lost during an absence. Pay is docked for tardiness. Since employees are paid by the hour and not salaried, no pay is awarded for days absent. Overtime must then be requested. After each chapter is completed and checked by the student, a test is requested. $10 times the percent correct is paid for each test taken. Those tests worth less than $6 may be retaken. All test earnings are recorded as overtime.

An accountant is hired for two class periods every two weeks. The accountant must collect time sheets (all overtime and test earnings must be initialed by the company president), secure tax tables, and calculate each employee's gross and net pay for the payroll period. The accountant is instructed to shortchange the employees. Whatever he or she makes that is undetected by the employee after two days is split with the company president. The intent here should be clear— to get students to use tax tables accurately and to check their paychecks. This becomes a real game for teens, even $.01 errors are challenged!

Student reaction has been overwhelmingly positive over the past eight years toward the entire simulation experience. Initially, in 1976, this course was a dumping ground, but now a variety of students enroll and are amazed at what they learn. Their suggestions for improvement always include extending the work simulation to the entire year or at least to the last semester.

Spalt, Inc. has allowed students, some for the first time ever, to bring to their math class a wealth of practical and specialized job knowledge and vocabulary. (Some of my students are concurrently enrolled in the area vocational center and others are planning to attend the next year or enroll in post-secondary vocational schools.) I ask for their help in interpreting the problems and ask them about the realism of some of the problems encountered—e.g., can a crankshaft really turn "X" rpms? They bring the practical experience and I bring the mathematics, which makes for a successful marriage. For other students, exposure to the vocabulary of mathematics as used in a vocation is an exciting experience. They see the real need for mathematics. I do very little selling, because I designed the course for those students whose learning style can be expressed as, "If I can see it, I can do it!" These kids generally do not do well in the traditional mathematics courses taught at our high school, in part because they do not see the applications of the theory. On the other hand, they do some quite sophisticated mathematics in the applied course—levels of algebra 2 and trigonometry—and enjoy it. In fact, it is amazing to observe how well these kids do with the trigonometry. I've taught the same unit to honors algebra students and I've found that my applied students do a much better job on the applied problems than the algebra students.

Sandra Spalt teaches mathematics at Red Bud High School in Red Bud, Illinois. The Red Bud program is well known in Illinois for its consistently excellent showings in state mathematics competitions. For further information on Spalt, Incorporated, contact:

Sandra Spalt
Red Bud High School
Red Bud, IL 62278

REFERENCES

Ewen, et al. **Career Mathematics.** Chicago: Merrill Publishing.

Gregg. **Basic Mathematics Skills.** New York: McGraw-Hill.

Haines. **Math Principles for Food Service Occupations.** Albany: Delmar Publishing.

I.R.S. **Understanding Taxes.** I.R.S. Data Center, Project K.I.T., P.O. Box 1200, Detroit, MI 48232.

Levine. **Vocational-Technical Math in Action.**

Lyng, Meconi and Zwick. **Career Mathematics: Industry and the Trades,** Boston: Houghton-Mifflin.

Mathematics of the Shop. Albany: Delmar Publishing.

Olivo and Olivo. 1953. **Basic Mathematics Simplified.** Albany: Delmar Publishing.

Pickar. **Dosage Calculations.** Albany: Delmar Publishing.

Practical Problems in Mathematics for: Automotive Technicians, Carpenters, Electricians, Machinists, Masons, Plumbers, Printers, Sheet Metal Technicians, Office Workers, Consumers, Metric System. Albany: Delmar Publishing.

Singer. **Mathematics at Work: Fractions; Mathematics at Work: Decimals; Mathematics at Work: Algebra.** New York: McGraw-Hill.

Smith. **Vocational-Technical Mathematics.** Albany: Delmar Publishing.

STRAIN YOUR BRAIN

by Jane M. Kessler

This is a game I have used to capture the attention of the class on those days that students usually don't feel like doing any work. The day before a vacation period is a good time.

These games are suitable for high school students of all ability levels, as the material can be easily modified to meet their needs. The complexity of the statements should be related to the ability level of the class.

All students are familiar with the old guessing game which starts, "I am thinking of a number between 1 and 10." The game can be extended to, "I am thinking of a number between 1 and 100." Play this once or twice with the class. Make note of the fact that in the second game, numbers 1 to 100, it is harder to guess the number unless some hints or clues are given. Play the game saying "higher" or "lower" after each guess. On the chalkboard, record the number of tries it takes for a student to guess the number without any clues compared to when clues are given.

Explain to the class that you are going to play a more sophisticated game called "Strain Your Brain." In this game a clue will mean a mathematical statement that has one or more solutions. These solutions will provide possible answers. However, unlike the guessing game you have just played, you won't be saying "higher" or "lower" after each guess. Instead, the students will have to determine if any of the clues contradict each other, and if so, to tell you.

First, let's try a few examples:
Clue 1: I am thinking of an even number.
Clue 2: The number I am thinking of solves the equation $x+4=7$.

You will note that clue 1 produces an infinite set of even numbers, and clue 2 tells us the number I am thinking of is 3. Since 3 is not even, the clues contradict each other.

Let's try another example:
Clue 1: The number I am thinking of is less than 6.
Clue 2: The number is in the prime factorization of 154 ($2\times7\times11$). These clues don't contradict. There is one prime factor of 154, namely 2, that is also less than 6.

It is time to look at the rules for this game.

Rules

Strain Your Brain is played by trying to guess what three numbers I am thinking of. All I can tell you is all three numbers are different in the set of real numbers. There are 10 clues to help you. However, all the clues are NOT true. You must decide if any clues contradict each other. When you notice a contradiction, raise your hand and tell me which clues contradict. I'll tell you which one is true and which one is false. As soon as you know all three numbers, call them out.

If you are unable to guess the number right away and need another clue, I'll reveal some more information. The first clue is worth 100 points, the second 90 points, and so forth. An incorrect contradiction or a wrong guess results in a loss of five points.

It is necessary to be sure that students understand the vocabulary used in the clues. This I teach as part of my regular lesson. At the end of each game, I go back over the clues, step by step, calling on students to suggest ways they used to arrive at the correct answer and we review the mathematical terms used.

Initially, one or two students will quickly discover the missing numbers. I find many of the slower members of the class sitting back and letting the brighter ones do all the work. You can counteract this by using teams, where every member needs to work out the solutions and by asking a student, after the answer has been given, to tell you how s/he solved the clue. For example, if clue 2 states that "one of the numbers is a factor of 24," you might ask a student who appeared not to be playing along, to tell you how s/he solved that clue. The students soon learn that they all must participate.

Surprisingly, it is not always the brightest students who get the answer first. Many students are so cautious that they are afraid to take a chance on giving an answer or noting a contradiction. As you continue to play the game, the class will feel more at ease. This is when it is a good time to challenge the students to write some games of their own. Just remind students who express an interest in writing their own games that the clues must contradict. It is usually a good idea to have a false clue contradict another clue more than once.

Initially students will write very difficult games, so no one will be able to solve them. I allow a few students to be the teacher and soon it becomes apparent that the class is not very interested, as clues such as "All three numbers are either rational or irrational numbers" have too many solutions.

Here is the start of a typical game that a student in algebra I wrote:
1. All three numbers are integers.
2. Zero is not one of the numbers.
3. The sum of the three numbers is greater than 1.
4. All of the numbers have 1 as a factor.

Note that after four clues, you can't tell if there are any contradictions, nor do you have a finite set to choose your answer from. Also, what information is clue 4 telling you? Point this out to the class. I usually work individually with students and soon the games become much better.

Here is a game written by another student:
1. All three numbers are factors of 60 (1, 2, 3, 4, 5, 6, 10, 12, 15, 20, 30, 60).
2. The sum of the three numbers is 110.
Note that the numbers 20, 30, and 60 fit both clues and this was the correct answer. Only if one of the first two clues was false would the game have gone on.

Here is a game written by the same student after I had worked with him.
1. All three numbers are factors of 60 (1, 2, 3, 4, 5, 6, 10, 12, 15, 20, 30, 60).
2. Two numbers are even and one is odd.
3. The sum of the three numbers is even. (This contradicts clue 2. The sum of an even number and an odd number is odd. Clue 2 is true; clue 3 is false.)
4. The sum of the numbers is greater than 105. (The only possible solution is 20, 30 and 60. However, this contradicts clue 2, which we know is true; so either clue 4 is false or clue 1 must be false and our solution set isn't the set of factors of 60. Clue 4 is false and clue 1 is true.) Note how much better this game is. You have a possible solution set, and you know two numbers are even and one is odd.
5. The sum of the numbers is 47.

Now this game got really interesting. I had two students arguing that there were only two possible solutions: 2, 15 and 30; and 5, 12 and 30—and both had been guessed. Suddenly, the quietest girl in the room volunteered the correct solution: 12, 15 and 20. This taught the class a valuable point. It pays to keep looking for the solution, as the most obvious answer may not be the solution. Had no one guessed the correct solution, the next clue would be given.

I have noticed several positive outcomes as a result of playing these games. First, they enjoy being teacher for a math period. Second, they have developed a critical, more challenging outlook in understanding mathematical concepts. Third, the review of mathematical terms is no longer a chore. Also, students are quick to want to learn any new mathematical concepts that appear in my daily lessons, as they never know when a term or concept may appear in one of the clues in a later game.

On the following pages I have listed two games. The clues are given first. In parentheses, I have put the solution I expect the students to arrive at.

The game is suitable for average ability algebra students.

1. All three numbers are factors of 12 (1, 2, 3, 4, 6, 12).

2. None of the numbers is both even and prime. (This does NOT contradict clue 1 as there are other possible numbers, other than the number "2," from which to choose.)

3. All three numbers are odd. (This clue contradicts clue 1 as there are not three odd numbers which are factors of 12. When a student points this out, I would tell him that clue 1 is true and clue 3 is false.) The student now has a set of numbers from which to draw his answer.

4. The sum of the three numbers is 7. (This clue contracts clue 2. If the number "2" is not a choice, then there are not three numbers whose sum is 7. Clue 2 is false, and clue 4 is true.)

5. One number is neither prime nor composite. (The number 1 is the correct answer.)

6. One number solves this equation: $x+8=10$. (The answer is 2. This contradicts clue 2. If a student noticed this, I would tell him/her clue 2 is false and clue 6 is true.) Remember, every student may not have seen the contradiction in clue 4.

7. All of the numbers are greater than 2. (This contradicts clues 5 and 6. Clues 5 and 6 are true and clue 7 is false.)

8. One number is $= \sqrt{16}$. (The correct answer is 4.)

9. One number is the smallest natural number. (The answer is 1. This contradicts clue 7. When a student notices this, tell him/her clue 7 is false and clue 9 is true.)

10. Two of the numbers are even and one is odd.

The correct answers are 1, 2, and 4.

The following game is suitable for students who have studied geometry.

1. All three numbers are the degree measure of angles of an acute triangle. (An acute triangle has all angles greater than zero, but less than 90 degrees.)

2. One number is the number of degrees in the supplement of an angle of 30°. (This contradicts clue 1. The supplement of 30° is 150°, and an acute triangle has all angles less than 90°. Clue 1 is true and clue 2 is false.)

3. None of the angles is greater than 70°.

4. Two of the measures of the angles are equal to 100°. (This contradicts clue 3. Clue 3 is false and clue 4 is true. The student should now know that one number is 80.)

5. All three numbers are multiples of 20. (If a student assumes that this clue is true, it is possible to guess the three numbers. According to the rules, all three numbers must be different so 80, 80, 20 is not a possible solution.)

6. One number is odd. (This contradicts clue 5 as there are no multiples of 20 which are odd. Clue 5 is true and clue 6 is false.)

7. One number solves this equation: $\sqrt{3600} = x$. (The answer is 60.)

8. The sum of the largest and the smallest number is equal to 120, and their difference is equal to 40. (Solving these equations simultaneously gives:

$$
\begin{aligned}
x + y &= 120 \\
\underline{x - y =\ \ \ 40} \\
2x &= 160 \\
x &= 80 \\
y &= 40
\end{aligned}
$$

9. None of the numbers could be the degree measure of an angle of an equilateral triangle. (An equilateral triangle has 60°. This contradicts clue 7. Clue 7 is true and clue 9 is false.)

10. The smallest number is 40.

The numbers I am thinking of are 40, 60, and 80.

TEACHING MATHEMATICS

Jane M. Kessler teaches mathematics in grades nine through twelve at Cheshire High School in Cheshire, Connecticut. For further information about her mathematics game, contact:

Jane M. Kessler
Cheshire High School
525 South Main Street
Cheshire, CT 06410

USING MATHEMATICAL SOFTWARE— ENRICHMENT OR RESTRICTION?

by Mona Fabricant

Is mathematical software the panacea of the 1980s? What function does it really serve? Is it a substitute for the teacher in the classroom? Is it a supplement to what is taught in the classroom? Is it enrichment or is it a self-paced approach for students? Does the use of mathematical software allow the teacher more time for individualized instruction?

Reading the literature on the use of mathematical software and the claims made for it by the publishing companies, all of the above questions would seem to be answered in the affirmative. As Computer Laboratory Coordinator and classroom teacher, I feel the true answer to the question of where mathematical software fits into the curriculum is more complex than implied by the simple questions above.

For the past three years I have had the opportunity to use mathematical software as part of regularly scheduled classroom work and as an outside class activity for students who need extra help. In particular, I have used arithmetic, algebra, and statistical software. Regardless of the subject matter, tutorial software can be divided into four types, each type having one or more specific objectives. I have categorized the software we have in the laboratory into Teaching Software, Exercise-Generating Software, Student-Generated Software, and Test-Generating Software. To use software effectively, it is important to understand what each type of software purports to do and how well it carries through on its goals.

Teaching Software

The first type of software, which I will call Teaching Software, has two objectives. It claims to teach a concept and to provide practice using that mathematical idea. The concept to be taught is presented using an approach chosen by the programmer or publisher. Many times this approach is dictated by the logistics of writing the program as opposed to pedagogical efficacy.

Most software does not come with a companion manual or textbook, although this seems to be changing. Many publishers are in the process of providing at least a practice manual to accompany the disk. Much of the literature points to the fact that teacher methodology is greatly influenced by the textbook used for the course. The lack of coordination between textbooks and teaching software results in the student encountering two completely different methodologies, one in the classroom and one in the computer laboratory.

If the students are using the software for a review session, the difference in approach leads to a lack of reinforcement of what was taught in the classroom. If the teacher wants to use the program to teach the concepts, then he or she must follow the dictates of the program in terms of methodology. On the other hand, if the students are using the software for extra help, it can be argued that a different approach is just what is needed to clear up the misunderstandings the students have. In practice, I have found that for the poorer math student, the need for consistency in methodology overrides the advantages of a second look at how to solve a particular type of problem. The end result is that the use of software with a different viewpoint from the one preferred and used by the classroom teacher can be confusing and frustrating for the student and restricting for the teacher.

Putting aside the problem of a conflict in pedagogical approach, the next point to consider is the type and number of exercises provided by the program. Because of the large amount of storage needed on the disk for some tutorial programs, exercises are limited to a point where the students find the program useless after a few times through it. Since the same problems are repeated again and again, the exercises provided no longer test the students' skills but rather their memory. Some software generate random problems and therefore do provide an abundant number of examples for the students. Although this solves the problem of providing enough variation in exercises, another problem crops up at this point. It is necessary to look at how the students are required to interact with the computer in terms of entering their solutions.

The first problem the student encounters in interacting with the software is figuring out what the machine is looking for. Take, for example, a tutorial disk in long division. One disk requires the student to enter the answer to the problem digit by digit, the program responding "right" or "wrong" after each entry. A second disk expects the student to enter the complete quotient. Neither of these programs told the student what was expected. To further confuse the student, some programs assume rounding to certain place value and therefore 2.3 will evoke "TRY AGAIN" when the machine is seeking 2.29. To be told that an answer is incorrect—and then redo the problem 3 or 4 times and not be able to understand why your correct solution is incorrect according to the computer—can destroy what little confidence the student has gained. The students usually catch onto these quirks of the program after a few examples, but the initial experience can leave them a little shaky.

The question now arises as to how many chances the machine will allow the student to try to get the correct answer. Some programs allow only one try and then either give the student the answer or just go on to another problem. Students usually do not like to be so restricted. A large number of programs allow the student three or four tries before giving the correct solution. This seems to be a reasonable approach. Unfortunately, I have seen some programs with an endless loop. The students cannot move on to another problem or part of the program until they somehow answer the present problem correctly. No help is provided even after five tries. If the student cannot get the correct answer on his own, he is forced to return to the very beginning of the program. Usually students encountering this situation just give up in frustration.

Another point to consider is whether the student is asked to work out the solution on the screen or with paper and pencil. Some programs have the student use the keyboard as the writing instrument and some have the student use paper and pencil. At this point, I do not have enough experience with using the keyboard as a writing tool for students to make a judgment as to which approach has the most benefits. Since some of the newest programs I have seen are using the keyboard approach, research has to be done in this area.

Teaching Software can be subcategorized as diagnostic and nondiagnostic. Diagnostic software will tell students where their errors are and/or why particular mistakes were made. In the ideal situation, the program then asks the students whether they would like additional problems of the same type or whether they prefer to go back and restudy the applicable tutorial section or sections. Most software does not fall into this category. Usually the student will have the option of going back page by page or continuing with more examples. For many students the most helpful approach, from their point of view, would be to redo the problem they answered incorrectly, followed by the option of returning to the appropriate tutorial material if necessary. To make the situation worse, a large percentage of the available software provides no diagnostics at all. In this case, the student has to continue trying examples and figure out what he or she is doing wrong or choose to go back to the beginning of the teaching program and reread the whole sequence. The students find neither of these alternatives satisfying.

Exercise-Generating Software

A second category of software has as its objective generating problems for practice. I will call this class of software Exercise-Generating Software. This software can also be subcategorized into diagnostic and nondiagnostic. The former kind of program points out where the student has made an error and then allows him or her to redo the problem or a similar problem. Unfortunately, most software just tells the student when he or she is right or wrong and generates another problem.

There are a number of positive aspects to Exercise-Generating Software. This software does NOT present a specific methodology. Therefore, it bypasses the problem of incompatibility between disk and textbook present in much of the Teaching Software. The important thing to look for is an easy-to-follow menu with enough subdivisions to withstand the impact of class-to-class differences in topic choices, as well as shifts in topic emphasis due to a change in textbook. An added bonus to look for is graded exercises.

The positive benefit for students is the opportunity to practice a mathematical skill they have acquired. This software, if it generates enough problems, provides practice with immediate feedback. This is different from using a textbook or problem sheet with an answer key. The computer can provide a more personal and motivating approach. For example, some software will encourage the student by use of phrases such as "Well done, Lauren" or "Dynamite job, Eric." Other programs will keep score of the number of correct answers the student gives. Software that keeps a running tally of the number of questions tried and the number completed correctly can also benefit the teacher in that the software can be used as self-graded exams.

Student-Generated Software

A third class of software is Student-Generated Software. The students write their own programs either to compute formulas or solve certain problems. For discovery learning and enrichment, student-written software can provide a method for testing mathematical conjectures and theories and coming to conclusions. A goal of this type of software is to have the student develop the necessary algorithm for solving a problem. Having to write a logical, structured program should force the student to think through the steps necessary to find a solution. For some students, this approach is helpful though, as the following example illustrates, caution is warranted. Assume the student is asked to write a program to use the quadratic formula to find the roots of a second degree polynomial. When the roots are equal, the discriminant should be zero. For certain values of x, however, x-squared is not computed exactly by the micro and, therefore, although the discriminant is close to zero, it is not exactly zero. Obviously this situation requires the student to change the algorithm or the format of the formula to overcome this obstacle, a sophisticated challenge that can result in undue frustration for the student.

Another consideration is that students come to class with different levels of programming proficiency and sometimes even different languages. If the programming involved in writing an algorithm becomes too complicated, the student can get so bogged down in the logic that he or she loses sight of the mathematical concept involved. There are some benefits to be derived by writing a difficult program in the classroom as a class, and then having the students run the program by hand (desk-edit). This forces the student to follow the computer's logic step-by-step. Some students can translate this knowledge into a viable method for working out the problems without using a computer.

Test-Generating Software

Another type of software is Test-Generating Software which is usually aimed at the teachers but can be used to generate practice problems for the students. This software succeeds in that it cuts down teacher test preparation time. It allows teachers to write many versions of the same exam or construct practice or homework sheets quickly. Also, the chore of writing make-up exams is lessened. It provides for more uniformity in tests, as well as better coordination between practice problems and test problems. If you decide to buy this type of software, look for an easy-to-use menu with many subdivisions and, if possible, graded questions.

To summarize, there is software that purports to teach, software that is aimed at providing practice, student-written software that is supposed to help clarify mathematical algorithms in the students' minds, and software to lessen the amount of time teachers have to spend preparing exams. Although each type of software can find a place in the curriculum, the limitations must be duly noted and taken into consideration.

Classroom Organizational Structures

Now that I have given you an overview of the tools at hand, let us look at what happens when they are used in different settings.

The first attempt we made at using software was a remedial tutor for students having problems in the classroom. These students were encouraged by their classroom teachers to use their free periods to go to the computer lab and work on the topics they were having trouble with.

In an ideal situation, the software would coordinate exactly with the textbooks used in the classroom in terms of vocabulary and pedagogical approach. However, this is the real world and since our lab is in the real world and since we have a tight budget, we bought software from whatever source seemed cheapest or most readily available. Even if we tried to stick with one publisher, however, they did not usually provide software encompassing the range of topics we required. Furthermore, either the publishers did not have coordinating texts available or, if they were available, they did not fit into our curriculum exactly as we needed. The result was an eclectic assortment of programs. The reality was that the classroom teacher usually presented material with a certain approach and specific vocabulary, and the disks presented a different method and/or vocabulary. For some students this was a bonus in that they could see the problems from a second point of view. As I indicated earlier, for many students it was just confusing.

The second major problem we found with our uncoordinated assortment of software was the great variety of directions for using the programs—for example, arrows were used to continue some programs, the space bar for others, and so on. Sometimes the same program had more than one set of directions. For each disk the student had to familiarize himself or herself with the directions before attempting to learn or practice the mathematical concept contained on the disk. For some students this meant that a large chunk of their time was spent adjusting to the disks' requirements before they could accomplish their original goals. For other students this situation proved too frustrating, and they did not make use of the computer facilities at all.

In order to try to lessen the negative and enhance the positive effects of the available software, we experimented with holding one session of the class per week in the computer lab, with the teacher present to give assistance. Since the teacher could fill in for these deficiencies, this approach was intended to eliminate the problems of inflexible answer formatting and nondiagnostic problem generating disks.

In classes where the number of students was less than or equal to the number of computers and available disks, things seemed to go better. Students were able to question the computer's responses and ask why they had gotten an incorrect answer. Of course, this assumes that a "period of awe" had passed, which usually took about two weeks, in which the students refused to question the machine's answer because "the computer is always correct."

In classes where the number of students was greater than the number of machines and students had to share, there were problems with concentration on the task at hand and conflicts over the different paces at which paired students sometimes worked. At times this problem was offset by the students helping each other. Unfortunately, if one of the pair was lazy, then he or she could get through class without doing very much work.

Even with the teacher present, the differences in methodology between the computer instruction and the classroom instruction caused confusion for some students. In order to avoid this lack of pedagogical coordination between human and machine, the instructor would have to spend quite a few hours in the lab going through each disk and writing lesson plans so that the vocabulary and methodology matched that of the available software, a demand of extra time and effort from teachers that is unfair considering their normal heavy load and responsibilities.

Although this paper may seem negative in its look at the impact of software on the curriculum, that is not really the impression I want to leave with the reader. Mathematical software has a definite place in the curriculum. It is not a panacea for remedial students, nor will it fill in all the gaps for the brighter student who needs enrichment.

For many of our students the computer as tutor has provided a nonjudgmental teacher. They enjoyed the unpressured atmosphere and spent many more hours doing math than they had in the past. The computer went at a pace that was comfortable for individual students, and they could reread the directions or the problems as many times as necessary.

The negative remarks about using software were made so that other teachers might avoid some of the pitfalls that I have encountered, and also so that the publishers will produce software that is student effective rather than just supposedly user friendly.

I will continue to use software to provide remedial help for students. I will also use software as an integral part of classroom instruction for presenting topics that require iterative procedures better done by machine than people, and I will encourage students to use available software to expand their knowledge. At the same time I will keep in mind the restrictions the computer imposes on my teaching. If you are presently in the process of evaluating software, keep these restrictions in mind also and carefully look at the disks for methodology, directions for using the program, branching and diagnostic ability, and answer formatting. In this way, the computer can become integral to your teaching, too.

Mona Fabricant is Assistant Professor of Mathematics and Computer Lab Coordinator at Queensborough Community College in New York. For further information about using mathematical software, contact:

Mona Fabricant, Ed.D.
Queensborough Community College
56th and Springfield Boulevard
Bayside, NY 11364

MATHEMATICS *DARES* IN THE OKLAHOMA CITY PUBLIC SCHOOLS

by Stan Hartzler

If knowledge is to be useful to the student for application or further learning, it must be knowledge that can be recalled. The mission of educators is to impart useful knowledge. It is not enough, therefore, that students explore a new idea one day, practice that idea only within close time proximity to the initial exploration, and then go on to another idea the next day, without trying to recall what was learned the previous days. Students must learn to recall with a "cold" mind, after passage of time and interruption of unrelated activity. When knowledge can be recalled after interruption, it is available and useful for further learning and application.

Two kinds of learning or learning stages must be achieved for knowledge to become useful: initial learning, and learning to recall what was once learned. Deliberate practice to accomplish cold recall must be provided on a daily basis, say the specialists on forgetting.[1,2] But, teacher time and burdens being what they are, few teachers do more than what is provided by textbooks, and textbooks heavily emphasize initial learning over recalled learning. Students rarely are presented problems or exercises which ask them to recall—"Oh, yeah, how DID we do that?" Most students practice problems only for initial learning, only shortly after teacher explanation.

DARES to Balance

The imbalance of attention to the two types of learning described above can be ended effectively by the development of materials, including textbooks, which invite cold recall on a daily basis. Almost any teacher or school district can facilitate systematic recall practice and review with little investment of time and money, and can tailor such practice to objectives chosen by teacher, district, and state. A program called DARES, begun in 1984 in Oklahoma City Public Schools for mathematics, exemplifies the makeup of such materials, how students and teachers benefit, and how such a program can be locally developed with little expense or trouble.

DARES is an abbreviation for Daily Assorted Review Exercise Set. These sets can be used in a variety of mathematics courses from elementary through secondary levels. An example of a four-day sequence of DARES for arithmetic appears in figure 1. The reader is encouraged to examine this illustration before reading further.

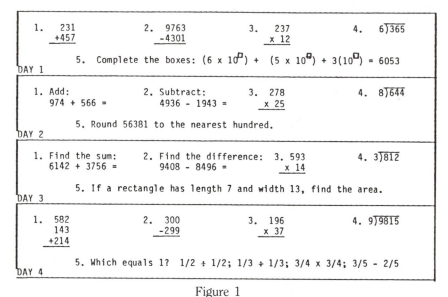

Figure 1

The First Four Day of a DARES Sequence for Arithmetic

As illustrated in figure 1: **a DARES consists of several questions or problems which are related to previously presented, widely varied course topics (one problem per topic within the set), the set being related by strategic similarity and contrast to other DARES in a day-to-day sequence.**

In figure 1, the first day's DARES consists of one addition problem, one subtraction problem, one multiplication problem, one division problem, and one noncomputational problem. The second day's DARES consists of different examples of the same variety of problems, and so on. Problems gradually become more difficult, and topics shift in and out of the sets as the sequence moves through the year. Where the typical daily textbook exercise allows for practice of one topic only, a DARES invites practice of different kinds of problems within a few minutes' time, allowing the student to practice "gear-shifting" between the various kinds of problems.

The following procedure is used:

1. DARES is given to the student **as a set,** on the blackboard, flip chart, overhead, ditto sheet, or (optimally) the textbook page. Teacher revision is invited so long as the set remains an assortment of different kinds of problems.

2. Students work uninterrupted on the DARES for 2-3 minutes while the teacher does some classroom management (attendance, returning graded papers). The teacher does not help any student until all have had the chance to attempt DARES **as a set.**

3. The teacher does the problems for the students as review instruction, aloud but at the teacher's speed. Answer keys are NOT provided, to help ensure that this important step is done.

4. Papers are collected for an effort grade. Teachers might collect papers prior to step 3 as needed for motivation for credible evaluation and ongoing diagnosis, or students might exchange papers.

5. Regular class work begins. Once established, the DARES routine should be finished 5-6 minutes after the beginning of the period.

6. Exams (if used) should be comprehensive, covering material throughout the year, with students informed of this policy at the beginning of the course.

What's the Difference?

DARES differs from other traditional instructional components in that fairly extensive review is provided briefly each day. In addition, instruction and practice on specific topics is extended over longer periods of time, and questions or problems are presented daily in close proximity to other types of questions or problems. Thus, a student is expected daily to recall facts, skills, concepts, or heuristics in tougher situations than the initial learning practice sets and chapter reviews of textbooks, which are the types most often done by students. The higher expectation of cold recall, communicated daily and supported by daily practice and feedback, produces the more secure knowledge that students inherently need.

Much research in educational psychology supports these changes over traditional textbook and classroom expectations. Related findings and principles assert that most forgetting occurs within 24 hours of initial learning,[1] and that most of what is learned is forgotten in 24 hours.[2] Also, within a given amount of practice time, or within a set number of exercise problems, numerous brief, widely-spaced practice sessions produce better gains than one or two practice sessions of greater duration.[3] Further, short-term retention is enhanced in at least one type of situation by back-and-forth practice on new and old topics,[4] and long-term retention is aided by review.[5] (The term "review," as opposed to "repetition," implies the passage of time between practices on a particular topic.) Turning back in the book to varied lessons to find varied problems is clumsy to implement and not helpful to achievement or retention.[6,7] Finally, concept formation is facilitated by presentation of related but contrasting ideas side-by-side on a daily basis.[8]

DARES to Benefit

Obvious benefits of using DARES include maintenance of skills for easier learning of more advanced ideas based on these prerequisites, as well as for minimizing reteaching. Student recall of the concept of place value facilitates learning of basic computation skills. Fourth-grade teachers are often frustrated in teaching long division to students who have forgotten how to subtract. Fifth-grade students can learn decimal division more easily if whole-number division has been practiced recently. The concept underlying the vertical positioning of decimal points in decimal addition or subtraction—namely, the need to add or subtract like kinds—is more easily understood and can be remembered by association if the student can recall the same need for common denominators when common fractions are added or subtracted. For students who can recall how to add algebra fractions, the popular process of developing the quadratic formula from $ax^2+bx+c=0$ can be very exciting and satisfying; students who cannot recall how to add $-c/a$ and $b^2/4a^2$ are often lost even after teacher assistance, and are left to acceptance of the quadratic formula as something found in a book, developed by someone else with a superior intellect (or so the students think). Sufficient review removes such stumbling blocks to advanced ideas and enjoyment in learning and doing mathematics.

Serendipitous benefits include ongoing diagnosis (especially helpful for midterm transfer students) and the increased likelihood for some daily success and consequent positive attitude toward self and subject. Teachers whose students move from room to room when classes change can easily direct students to a DARES task at the beginning of the period. Studies clearly demonstrate the supreme importance of the first few minutes of class time for getting students involved with the subject content.[9] Joanne Rogers, a fourth-grade teacher at Putnam Heights Elementary, expected her students to start each DARES every day upon entering the room. "They had time to finish during attendance, lunch count, etc. This kept the children quiet during a frustrating time of day; it also provided good instruction for the children and was easy for the teacher to do." Among many teachers agreeing is Judith Castleberry of Lee Elementary School. "DARES not only provides daily review, but the children coming into the classroom know exactly what to do. This keeps them 'on task' from the minute they get to class and they have less tendency to misbehave."

More than one casual observer has speculated that daily review would be boring, especially for better students. Most experienced teachers disagree. Richard Rhoad, a mathematics instructor at New Trier East High School in Winnetka, Illinois, has taught and coached some of the finest high school mathematics contestants in the United States, and he insists that even his best students need review daily. The geometry book he co-authored provides review problems throughout for topics in algebra, arithmetic, and previously covered geometry. Teachers commonly report that the best students love to show off and are the most noticeably angry at themselves when they err in the daily review.

Ron Poole, mild-mannered principal at Harding Middle School, recalls a day when he was "downright rude" to several people wanting to stop him as he attempted to get to a formal observation of a new teacher's class before the tardy bell rang. Poole succeeded, he thought, until he entered the classroom and found everyone in place and working on the DARES. He sat down and was still fuming that he had apparently failed to hear the tardy bell, when the tardy bell rang. "The students actually run to class to get started," said another Harding math teacher. Not surprisingly, the Harding MATHCOUNTS team placed third in Oklahoma state competition, no small achievement in a year (1985) when the Oklahoma state team placed third in the national MATHCOUNTS competition.

What's the News?

Readers familiar with educational research, especially research on implementation of ideas in general and on the most beneficial pacing of practice and review, are apt to say at this point that the foregoing is nothing new. This assessment is correct. My message has been said many times before. However, these ideas are not routinely used by a majority of teachers and publishers.

What is new, then, is that materials exist which, if used, effect implementation of the ideas; more materials can easily be developed; teachers in large numbers are learning to improve on textbooks; the principles are being used in spite of inadequate teacher training with respect to review; and there is real potential for commonly greater mathematics achievement than in the recent past.

Doing DARES

A handful of textbook authors have incorporated DARES characteristics with the exercises which routinely follow each day's discussion of new material. Most notable of these authors is John Saxon.[9,10,11,12.] Rhoad et al[13] and Hake[14] are to be counted among other authors who have incorporated DARES principles in daily exercise sets. Several school districts, notably the Dallas Independent School District, the San Antonio ISD, and the Freemont Union High School District in San Jose, have written year-long DARES sequences for each grade or course for mathematics.

DARES Aborning

The development of the first 40-day DARES sequence in Oklahoma City was for fourth grade mathematics. The idea was presented to 52 principals, who collectively suggested the names of 8 teachers who might be willing to volunteer help. Six of the teachers agreed to a meeting, to which four came. In one hour, the job was done. The process began with the decision to write a 40-day sequence of 5-problem DARES for an agreed-on scope and sequence. Each of the 5 persons then was assigned a type of problem and a problem number for each of the 40 sets. The problems in each set were, in order, addition, subtraction, multiplication, division, and application or problem solving, similar to those shown in each set in figure 1.

Forty sheets of paper were numbered consecutively. The person in charge of question 1 wrote an addition problem on sheet #1, and passed that sheet on to the person in charge of question 2, who contributed a subtraction problem to sheet #1. In this manner the 40 sheets were passed among the five people. Another volunteer teacher later copied the sets in condensed form, as in figure 1, to reduce the number of pages needing duplication.

From the first, teacher response was excellent. "Oh, THAT's what you've been telling us about! Good idea!" Third- and fifth-grade teachers borrowed copies. A seventh-grade committee wrote another 40-day sequence, to be used also by sixth grade, eighth grade, and high school teachers.

That summer (1984) saw much volunteering and the development of 120-day sequences for each of grades K through remedial high school. The program has been expanded again for school year 1985-86.

The district-level experiences mentioned above and feedback from the author's out-of-district presentations to thousands of teachers and administrators indicate that a program of DARES sequences is quickly perceived to be more than another Quick Fix. Certainly much development and refinement of the description, possible forms, and benefits of DARES remains to be done. Meanwhile, sufficient rationale, evidence, and capability exists for any school district to begin immediately and develop and use DARES sequences, and to argue for inclusion of this structure of student practice in commercially published curriculum materials.

Stan Hartzler is the Mathematics/Science Program Leader for the Oklahoma City Public Schools. For further information on his DARES program, contact:

Stan Hartzler, Ph.D.
Curriculum Services Department
Oklahoma City Public Schools
900 North Klein
Oklahoma City, OK 73106

REFERENCES

1. Horowitz, Leonard M. 1984. "Learning." **World Book Encyclopedia.**
2. Buzan, Tony. 1983. **Use Both Sides of Your Brain.** Dutton.
3. Woodworth, Robert and Harold Schlosburg. 1954 (and later editions). **Experimental Psychology.** Holt, Rinehart, and Winston.
4. Underwood, Benton J. 1983. **Attributes of Memory.** Scott Foresman.
5. Weaver, J.R. 1976. **The Relative Effects of Massed vs. Distributed Practice Upon the Learning and Retention of 8th Grade Mathematics.** Dissertation, the University of Oklahoma. (Contains summary of background and in-use evidence before 1976.)
6. Mora, Bob. 1983, 1984. Personal communications.
7. Robinson, James T. 1981. **Research in Science Education: New Questions, New Directions.** ERIC Clearinghouse for Science, Mathematics, and Environmental Education. Columbus, OH.
8. Johnson, David. 1983. **Every Minute Counts: Making Your Math Class Work.** Seymour Publications.
9. McBee, Maridyth. 1982. **Dolciani vs. Saxon: A Comparison of Two Algebra I Textbooks with High School Students.** Planning, Research, and Evaluation Department, Oklahoma City Public Schools, 900 North Klein, Oklahoma City, OK 73106.
10. Reed, Beverly Woods. 1983. **Incremental, Continuous-Review vs. Conventional Teaching of Algebra.** Dissertation, University of Arkansas.
11. Melvin, Ann. August 27, 1984. "A Man With a Mission." **Dallas Morning News.**
12. Lester, Mary. 1983, 1984. Personal communications.
13. Rhoad, Richard, et al. 1984. **Geometry for Enjoyment and Challenge.** Revised edition. McDougal, Littell & Company.
14. Hake, Stephen. (Series of textbooks.) Gidley School, El Monte, CA.

TEACHING THE EXPECTED WITH THE GEOMETRIC SUPPOSER AND MEETING THE UNEXPECTED

by Richard Houde and Michal Yerushalmy

> . . .This indicated to him a means of solving the problem and he did not delay, but in his joy leapt out of the tub, and rushing naked towards his home, he cried out with loud voice, "heureka, heureka."

Introduction

The story about Archimedes is known to many students; our culture has generalized it to represent the image of creation in the sciences. Unfortunately, the story does little to motivate students to think about themselves as inventors, or, in our case, as geometers. The Archimedes episode produced a stereotype of creation and the creator: creation is a propitious incident, and the chances of ingenuous mortals to be the lucky protagonists of such an event are slim; the creator is a queer, eccentric character, and you must be such a character to be able to invent.

During the first week we tried the Geometric Supposer, more than three years ago, a student said: "Now I understand how geometry was invented." This happened right after she and her friend conjectured about a property that was new to them, as well as to their teacher.

What was the connection between the two stories? For Archimedes, the tub became the tool he needed to find the solution to the "weight of the crown" problem. For our students, the Geometric Supposer produced a wealth of data, allowed them to conjecture about it, and extended an invitation for creation in geometry.

To understand the nature of creation is one thing; to fulfill the requirements of the high school geometry curriculum is another. This article will suggest a method of teaching geometry while watching for the expected and welcoming the unexpected.

The Geometric Supposer

For the past two years we have been working with students in four geometry classes of approximately 20 students each at Weston High School in Weston, Massachusetts. The students formed the second level of Weston's four-level tenth grade geometry program. We believe that with our guidance these students were able to behave like geometers and to create themselves a geometry curriculum based on conjecturing and problem posing. The primary tool used in this task was the Geometric Supposer, an innovative computer program published by Sunburst Communications for the Education Development Center in Newton, Massachusetts.

The Geometric Supposer allows the students to choose a primitive shape such as a triangle or a quadrilateral, and then to make any construction that Euclid knew how to make. The program remembers the construction as a procedure that can be carried out on any other shape within the same primitive. Using this technique, any construction with different types of triangles or quadrilaterals may be examined quickly and easily.

The Geometric Supposer allows the construction of points, segments, circles, parallels, perpendiculars, angle bisectors, and extensions of line segments. When the primitive shape is a triangle, it allows construction of medians, midsegments, altitudes and perpendicular bisectors. The program includes options to label various types of points such as intersection points, random points (on, outside and inside shapes), reflections of points and line segments. Points and line segments can be easily erased. Besides procedural constructions, the program can measure angles and lengths of line segments, compute the perimeters and areas of triangles and quadrilaterals, divide segments into sections of equal length, and make scale drawings.

As will be shown below, the Geometric Supposer can encourage students to behave like geometers because of the wealth of visual and numerical data it provides, and because conjectures about relationships observed within the data can be quickly tested. (Naturally, the students' conjectures can be stated as theorems only after they have been formed, numerically tested, and formally proven.) More important, the measurement capabilities of the program allow students to find counterexamples for given conjectures easily, and help them understand the important role counterexamples play in the scientific process.

Suppose, for example, that a student, using the Geometric Supposer, draws a median in an isosceles triangle from the vertex angle to its opposite side, and conjectures that the median bisects the vertex angle. The student can measure the angles in question and test the conjecture further by drawing other isosceles triangles and performing similar measurements. Data obtained in this way forms the basis for a conjecture that the student believes is true; a formal geometric proof will change this conjecture into a theorem.

Now suppose that the student goes further and conjectures that a similar idea holds true for all triangles, that is, a median drawn from the vertex of any triangle to the opposite side bisects the angle. When this conjecture is tested, counterexamples emerge readily. The student learns immediately that the conjecture is not true because at least one counterexample has been found.

The power of the Geometric Supposer is most evident when making conjectures related to complicated diagrams, where it allows students to test conjectures at great speed. For example, a student draws the three angle bisectors in an acute triangle, notices that they are concurrent, and surmises that this is true for all acute triangles. The Geometric Supposer allows the student to test this conjecture by repeating instantly the drawing of angle bisectors in other acute triangles, as many times as needed. For any conjecture, the Geometric Supposer allows students to construct numerous examples, far more than they would have the time or the desire to construct manually.

Classroom Practice

Traditionally, the teaching of high-school geometry has emphasized the principles of deductive systems. This approach often forces students to learn how to manipulate mathematical systems, while denying them an equal opportunity to create geometry. Geometry teachers have always faced the dilemma of having to instill in their students an appreciation of deductive, mathematical systems, while at the same time offering them an opportunity to create mathematics. This section describes how these activities are combined in the classroom.

For two of every five available class periods, lectures were given on specific geometry topics that led to assigned worksheet and Supposer problems. Geometry textbooks were not distributed to the students until the second part of the third quarter. The class text consisted of lecture notes, worksheets with routine problems, and notebooks containing problem sets, lists of conjectures, and lists of theorems with their proofs. The remaining three class periods were spent using the Geometric Supposer in the school's computer lab or in "geometry seminars" where students presented the work they have done with the Geometric Supposer or sought help with worksheet exercises.

We found the seminars exciting because students presented the geometry they had developed, and they were talking about it. Students presented their conjectures, proofs, and counterexamples freely, and seemed to enjoy the intellectual arguments that often ensued.

Students worked on Supposer problems independently or in pairs, during and outside class time. Occasionally they asked for hints, or for a restatement of the problem. At times they were stumped by their inability to draw conclusions from their data and they would congregate to discuss their predicament. These conversations often resulted in a restatement of the problem, and students would go back to work. We found some of the best problems for the course while listening in on their conversations, or trying to answer their questions.

The Expected and the Unexpected

The traditional geometry curriculum contains what is assumed to be the minimum body of knowledge necessary for understanding the completeness of the Euclidean creation. We tend to forget that there are hundreds of problems and theorems that were probably known to any student in ancient Alexandria, which have long been forgotten. One may argue that our students can barely cope with the minimum, why burden them with new problems? Our experience in inductive learning with the Supposer suggests that a tool that makes conjecturing easy and provides an environment that encourages interesting creation, also brings students closer to what we assume to be their true ability.

We confronted the students with open-ended problems, describing a situation and occasionally suggesting directions for investigation, but never indicating that there was a single goal or idea to be pursued. Usually, but not necessarily, the content referred to traditional high school curriculum material. For example:

Draw a midsegment in triangle ABC and list as many conjectures as possible. Could you transform some of your conjectures into theorems?

This was a test problem that was allotted 45 minutes of independent work on conjectures. The students had not been exposed previously to the term "midsegment" stated in the problem, but knew that it was listed as an element in the "Draw" menu of the program. Some of the results were expected and are part of the traditional curriculum:

1. DE‖BC, DE=1/2 BC

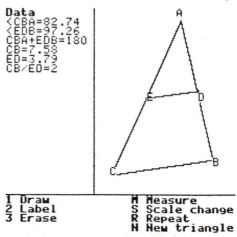

```
Data
<CBA=82.74
<EDB=97.26
CBA+EDB=180
CB=7.58
ED=3.79
CB/ED=2
```

```
1 Draw          M Measure
2 Label         S Scale change
3 Erase         R Repeat
                N New triangle
```

2. The distance from A to DE equals the distance between DE and BC.

3. If CD is a median in △ABC, and DF is parallel to CB, then DE is a midsegment.

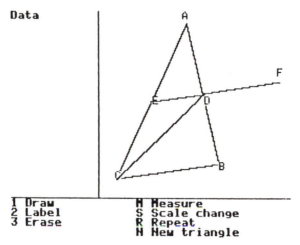

4. If △ABC is an isosceles (AB=AC) or an equilateral, and DE is a midsegment, then CDEB is an isosceles trapezoid.

5. DECF, BDFE and DAFE are parallelograms with equal areas.

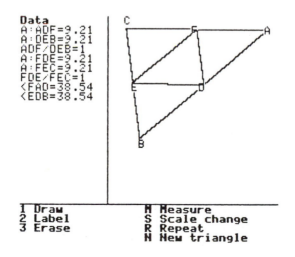

Other conjectures were not expected, and appeared to be inspired by earlier class discussions.

6. △ADF, △ABC, △DFE, △BED and △FEC are all triangles of the same type, with congruent angles. Note: this problem was assigned before similarity has been introduced.

7. If ABC is a right triangle, and DE is a midsegment, then ACE is an isosceles (EC=EA) and ∝(△ECD)=∝(△EAD). [∝=area]

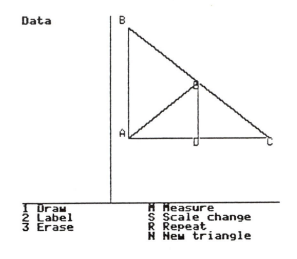

```
I Draw            H Measure
2 Label           S Scale change
3 Erase           R Repeat
                  N New triangle
```

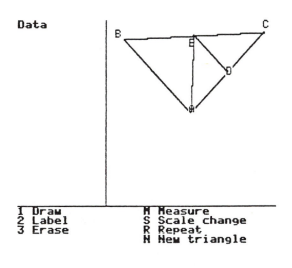

```
I Draw            H Measure
2 Label           S Scale change
3 Erase           R Repeat
                  N New triangle
```

Data

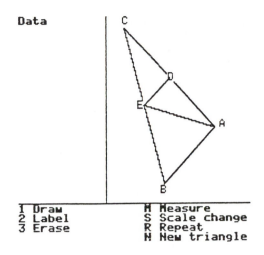

```
1 Draw          M Measure
2 Label         S Scale change
3 Erase         R Repeat
                N New triangle
```

8. In any △ABC, if ED is a midsegment and EB and AD are medians, then ∝(△CDE)=3 * ∝(△DEF) and the perimeter of △DEF=1/2 * perimeter of △AFB.

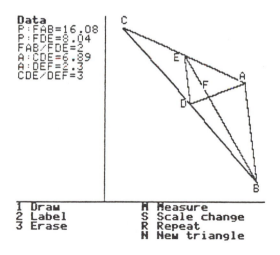

```
Data
P:FAB=16.08
P:FDE=8.04
FAB/FDE=2
A:CDE=6.89
A:DEF=2.3
CDE/DEF=3
```

```
1 Draw          M Measure
2 Label         S Scale change
3 Erase         R Repeat
                N New triangle
```

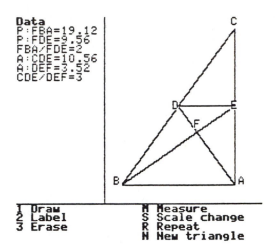

9. If DF is a midsegment in △ABC, and GH is a midsegment in △ADF, then HE and GE trisect FD in points I and J.

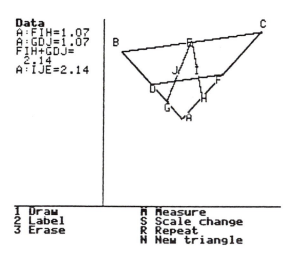

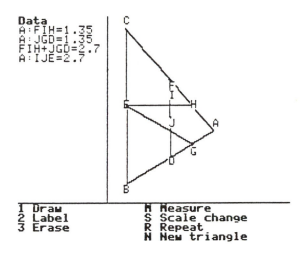

Also, $\propto(\triangle IJE) = \propto(\triangle DJG) + \propto(\triangle FIH)$.

The next example is a problem that one can often find in traditional geometry textbooks:

Divide the sides of a square ABCD into three equal parts and form an equilateral EGIK.

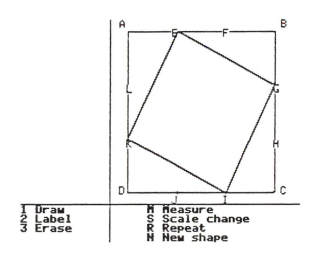

161

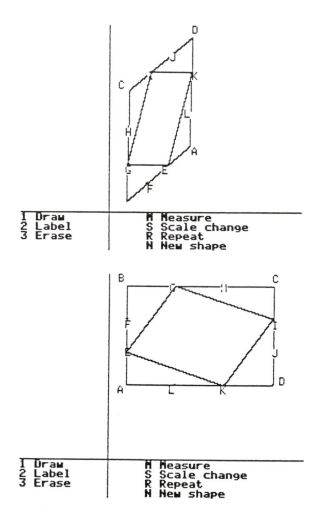

(a) EGIK is _____.

(b) Compare ABCD and EGIK with respect to areas, perimeters and lengths of sides. Any conjectures?

(c) Answer questions similar to those found in part (a) and (b) above for quadrilaterals other than a square, and state as many conjectures as possible.

What we usually ask students to do is to prove that EGIK is a square, using congruent triangles.

Students found that EGIK was a square and they also provided a proof that was motivated by unusual intermediate constructions:

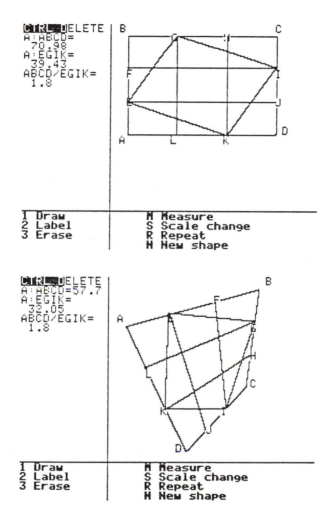

Another expected result was:
If ABCD is a parallelogram then EGIK is a parallelogram.

But these were a few unexpected conjectures and even more unexpected convincing arguments following the conjectures. The "grid" construction they added led them to the following conjecture: in all quadrilaterals the ratio between the two areas is 1.8! Or, the same phenomenon expressed differently:

$$\propto(ABCD) \ / \propto(EGIK) \ = \ 9/5.$$

Another type of "grid" was formed and followed by a different conjecture:

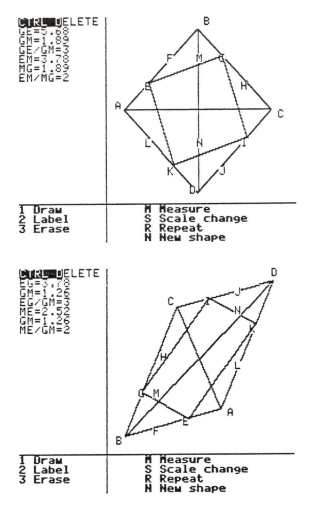

A diagonal of square ABCD divides a side of the inscribed square EGIK by a ratio of 1:2.

Teaching Conflicts

Teaching inductively forces the teacher to confront different methodology problems than those faced in traditional teaching. The following are some of the problems encountered, all having to do with unexpected answers:

1. There are too many conjectures, and the time does not allow the teacher to deal with all of them.
2. The conjecture is true but it is too difficult to prove in view of the students' present knowledge.
3. The conjecture is false.
4. The conjecture seems to be true but we can find neither a proof nor a counterexample.

All four situations involve the students' ability, in terms of time and understanding, to prove or to refute a conjecture.

Our experience suggests that these difficulties can be overcome. If the difference between a conjecture and a theorem has been made clear, there is no need to prove every conjecture. It is possible to develop "summarizing" techniques, using worksheets or the board, that will allow each student to obtain the conjectures of the others. Later in the course, when the students have acquired the appropriate background for handling a given conjecture, the teacher can bring up selected conjectures and attempt proving or refuting them.

By adopting such an approach to the learning, we grant students the freedom while retaining control over timing and curricular demands; we make students appreciate the deductive system by making them aware of the process that distinguishes between a hypothesis and a theorem; and we transform teaching into a high level intellectual experience, and eliminate the fear of having to confront the unexpected.

Conclusion

A teacher who contemplates using the Geometric Supposer as we did is unlikely to find a parallel example in high school mathematics classroom teaching today. The pedagogy we used most closely resembles the teaching ordinarily found in science classes, where the primary focus is on the scientific process of data collection, conjecturing, and finding counterexamples or generalizations.

We hope that this curricular and pedagogical approach will suggest new ways for teachers and students to approach the learning of geometry at the secondary school level. We encourage teachers who believe in this style of inductive learning to consider using the Geometric Supposer the next time they have the opportunity to teach geometry. Our experience demonstrated that students brought a high degree of enthusiasm to their work, and an ability to create geometry that we never thought possible.

Richard Houde is head of the mathematics department at Weston High School in Weston, Massachusetts. He has served as an advisor for Harvard's Educational Technology Center and for the Education Development Center in Newton, Massachusetts, where the Geometric Supposer was developed.

Michal Yerushalmy was one of the primary developers of this software. Currently she works at Education Development Center and the Harvard Graduate School of Education. For further information about the Geometric Supposer, contact:

Richard Houde
Weston High School
Weston, Massachusetts 02193

or

Michal Yerushalmy
Education Development Center
55 Chapel Street
Newton, Massachusetts 02160

ADVANCED PLACEMENT CALCULUS: THE FINAL THREE WEEKS

by Rita M. Thompson

Probably the most crucial period of an advanced placement calculus course occurs during the final three weeks. During this time, the teacher must summarize a year-long course and must make certain that the students have understood all the intricate, interconnecting concepts. The final three weeks of an AP calculus course are necessary for fine tuning or polishing the students' understanding of the calculus as a whole.

From past experiences, I have learned that high school students either do not know **how** to review for a comprehensive exam or do not possess the self-discipline to schedule their own study time. I have found more success with a strictly controlled, teacher-guided study schedule. All new concepts from the calculus syllabus should be presented before the last three weeks of the course. At that time, I begin an intensive review.

First, we must all understand the work, motivation, and time that will be demanded during this review. The teacher and the students must be totally committed to this effort. Following a motivational pep talk on the importance of this final thrust, we begin the review.

The first week we begin by summarizing the first two chapters. This is followed by a quiz. Students must fully realize that **all** work done during this review time will be checked for accuracy and will be assigned a grade. The third day, we review related rates, maximum/minimum problems, graphing, and conics. The following day, we take a quiz on these topics. Finally we review all the methods of integration; progress is measured by another short test.

While we are reviewing and taking quizzes, the students are expected to work on take-home projects. During the first week, they are required to work the 1979 AP calculus free response test and the 1969 multiple choice calculus exam. They are allowed to use their books and notes. At this point, it is essential that the students realize the objectives of this exercise. No matter how much help they must get, their consistent efforts on these former tests will force them to think about topics previously covered and possibly forgotten. At the very least, the students will have a better idea of the concepts that are still vague or confusing for them and will be encouraged to seek extra explanations. And at best, some will become more inspired to strive for scores of fives and fours on the advanced placement exam.

During the second week of review, the out-of-class assignments include the 1982 essay test and the 1973 multiple choice calculus exam. Some superior students usually are motivated to spend hours on these. Nevertheless, the fact that these tests will be graded will make the other, average students also do the work. All students are required to hand in their work. Thus, if one student does seek help from another person, he or she will still have to write the steps, and it is hoped that this will imprint in his or her memory the proper technique. The in-class activities for that second week include a discussion of the quizzes and take-home papers that were due the previous week. I do set aside one day to administer a standardized calculus exam published by the Educational Testing Service (©1964). This consists of a thirty-problem multiple choice exam with a forty-minute time limit. The test covers topics from first and second semesters and provides us with an opportunity to work on speed and accuracy. Few will completely finish, but all will learn how to pace themselves a little better.

Finally, we get to the last week before the advanced placement calculus exam. I have been fortunate in having my calculus class scheduled directly before lunch. This is always beneficial when my teacher-made tests are too long. In addition, this situation gives me a chance to administer the 1983 and the 1984 essay portions in the one hour-fifteen-minute time frame set by the advanced placement calculus exam. On two days of that last week, we brought lunches into class and attempted the two exams. Students developed a personal recognition of the topics and discovered how best to pace themselves. These papers were graded, returned, and discussed the following day.

We used the final day of class to wrap up last minute details. This is also the last official class time students will be able to ask questions from the take-home work and the classroom tests. I quickly reminded them of several concepts on the AP syllabus and warned them of problem areas that usually cause students difficulty. Over the years, it seems that maximum/minimum word problems and graphing functions including asymptoms, symmetry, and cusps have caused many problems for students. When we first touched upon these two topics during the school year, I slowed the class pace and spent extra time and practice to ensure the students' understanding and confidence about these two concepts. Recently, during the review weeks I have begun practice on graphing functions, when data or the graph of the function's derivative are given. I must admit that this is one of the most frantic question and answer sessions of the year.

My 1985 calculus class was quite unusual in that fourteen of twenty-three students asked if we could have a study session on Sunday, the day before the actual exam. One student offered her home as a meeting place and we studied together from 2:00 to 4:00 p.m. This afforded an opportunity to clarify any questions that had surfaced during the weekend while the students had been studying individually.

One must remember that these last three weeks of work are quite demanding and very intense. Since the take-home tests and the classroom quizzes/tests are all advanced placement questions, I do grade their work differently. I make certain that more than fifty percent of the required work is done in class (since there is no sure way of knowing what amount of the take-home tests was actually done by each student). Secondly, to calculate the student's grade, I find a percent, the total of points earned by the student divided by the total number of points that could possibly have been earned. (Each assignment or test was assigned a point value ranging from twenty points to forty-eight points.) Because the advanced placement material is truly college-level work, I assigned letter grades as follows:

$$90\%\text{-}100\% = A$$
$$80\%\text{-}\ 89\% = B$$
$$70\%\text{-}\ 79\% = C$$
$$60\%\text{-}\ 69\% = D$$
$$\text{Below}\ 60\% = F$$

(This is somewhat more lenient than my grading scale on teacher-made tests and quizzes throughout the year.) I hope this concession on my part shows that the classroom grade is not as important as their knowledge and their performance on the exam for college credit. This encourages them to study and to do their own work since the emphasis is on their **individual** success on the AP exam.

This time of year is the most demanding on the students and on the teacher. I give a sincere sigh of relief on the day of the AP calculus exam. However, the rewards of this type of review are clear to me. The following table summarizes the scores of former students who experienced this structured review. (Scores of three or higher are considered passing, with five being the highest possible score.)

	Number of Students Per Year		
Score	1983	1984	1985
5	6	5	11
4	6	6	7
3	6	6	4
2	0	2	1
1	1	0	0

Unstructured and open-ended written and oral course evaluations of the review weeks indicated that the students thought it was very intense but more helpful than if they had been working on their own. Many students learn math skills in a piecemeal, sometimes unconnected fashion. This structured review made the students see their calculus skills as a whole, integrated field. Some students wrote on their evaluations: "I didn't realize that I had learned anything until I reviewed for the AP exam. It is **amazing** how much I've gotten out of this class." Another said, "I thought the review was very intense, but it was effective and it helped me to expect what was going to be on the exam." A few students even admitted: "My lack of discipline is atrocious and I need to be forced to do a lot of things. Thanks so much for your **hard, hard** work..."

Of course, the most difficult part for me in teaching an advanced placement course is not the time, work, or stress of the daily teaching or review days. It is the waiting two months for the results.

This type of test review can be used in any other math course to induce students to work. By attaching a grade value to their efforts, most students are encouraged to work harder and thereby review better. Too often, a review day becomes a work day for the teacher and a day when students don't feel they must participate one hundred percent. The calculus review described above puts the work and the benefits in the student's lap. In fact, a review similar to the above one was tried in an algebra II class. Students had finished the course syllabus two weeks early. The teachers then systematically reviewed the first six weeks' material and tested on it, reviewed and tested the second six weeks' concepts and so on. The students' performance on their year-end, comprehensive exam was significantly higher. In addition, their readiness for a trig course the following fall was much better.

There are some words of warning to other teachers who may be considering a similar review. One must be prepared to dedicate many hours and much work in order to be successful. The teacher is the focal point, the one who is organized and demanding. Deadlines must be honored or a penalty imposed (for example, a deduction of points). This is the only way students can learn to set priorities for themselves, to be more self-disciplined. Be conscious of time limits.

Often students want extra time to continue working, but remember: standardized tests are exact on time limits. One suggestion is to give extra time on difficult tests during the first part of the school year and then start abiding by time limits in March and April to prepare students for the actual test.

I do not advocate "teaching for a test." In fact, I personally cover one and a half chapters that are not required by the AP syllabus. However, since the students will receive college credit after testing on certain concepts selected by the Advanced Placement Testing Committee, I think it is most beneficial for them to review as well as possible. My goal in using this review method is twofold: to aid the students to do their best work on the AP exam and to teach the students how to review by themselves for any year-long, comprehensive exam.

AP Calculus Class Schedule 1985

Thursday, April 18	Last test (on integration methods)
Friday, April 19	AP calculus contest for the Continental Math League; distribute 1979 essay test
Monday, April 22	Review chapters 1 and 2; distribute 1969 multiple choice take-home exam
Tuesday, April 23	Quiz on chapters 1 and 2
Wednesday, April 24	Review chapters 3 and 8
Thursday, April 25	Quiz on chapters 3 and 8; 1979 essay test is due
Friday, April 26	Review chapters 4, 5, 6, 7; distribute 1973 multiple choice take-home exam
Monday, April 29	Quiz on chapters 4, 5, 6, 7; 1969 multiple choice exam is due
Tuesday, April 30	Distribute 1982 essay exam
Wednesday, May 1	In-class standardized test (40 minutes)
Thursday, May 2	1982 essay test is due; distribute 1981 essay take-home exam
Friday, May 3	1973 multiple choice take-home is due
Monday, May 6	1983 essay test (in class) 1 hour and 15 minutes
Tuesday, May 7	1981 essay take-home is due; review 1983 essay taken on Monday
Wednesday, May 8	1984 essay test (in class) 1 hour and 15 minutes
Thursday, May 9	Review 1984 essay test
Friday, May 10	Return all old papers; final wrap-up
Monday, May 13	AP calculus exam, 8:00 a.m.

Rita M. Thompson teaches advanced placement calculus at Central High School in Memphis, Tennessee. For further information on her program, contact:

Rita M. Thompson
Central High School
306 South Bellevue
Memphis, TN 38104

IF YOU DON'T ASK THE RIGHT QUESTIONS, YOU DON'T GET THE RIGHT ANSWERS

by Jacqueline H. Simmons,
Deberah E. Perkins and Timothy R. Colburn

The "right answer" should not be the only concern of mathematics teachers and school administrators. Students must understand problems and have the ability both to analyze and solve them. For consistent performance and acquisition of skills in the application, analysis, synthesis, and evaluation of problems, students must receive direct instruction and practice in those areas. Therefore, let us examine some of the "right questions" that are relevant to these broadened concerns.

What activities do you prescribe if you wish to teach analytical thinking skills and problem solving? In the search for some activities that would assist students in analyzing and solving problems, we uncovered the Pair Problem Solving method. Pair problem solving is an instructional technique described in the book, **Problem Solving and Comprehension,** authored by Arthur Whimbey and Jack Lochhead. This technique involves two students, a problem solver and a listener, who work cooperatively to solve problems. One student thinks aloud while solving the problem; the other serves as listener, questioner, and certifier.

Since analysis and problem solving are generally invisible, we must be able to assess them and either modify or support them. We must also be able to provide these corrective or supportive activities for each student as often and as soon as new learnings occur. Describing the steps and strategies aloud makes the mental process apparent to the listener so that any errors can be detected and corrected. This is a central part of pair problem solving.

The problem solver expresses in words the steps taken in solving a given problem. The teacher must first model this procedure for the students, for it is an unfamiliar practice, and in the case of some students, a practice that has been discouraged. Students should be able to hear good problem solvers verbalize their thoughts as they work through step-by-step complex ideas and relationships.

The role of the listener is not passive. The listener demands constant verbalization from the problem solver and checks for accuracy at every step. The listener works along with the problem solver, asking questions, requiring clarification, and requesting elaboration. Although the listener never gives the right answer, every step taken and every conclusion reached is checked.

Group sizes other than pairs often are used. One of the important features of pair problem solving is that students work cooperatively to solve problems; so what originates as pair problem solving can be expanded into larger groupings involving "peer" problem solving, with all of the benefits intact, and even including some enhancements. The activity, the amount of time available, the number of students, all can make a larger size group more effective. Peer problem solving, then, involves two or more students working cooperatively to solve problems. In "pair" as well as "peer" problem solving, students analyze the process and the solution aloud, work together, and learn from each other.

When is peer problem solving used in the teaching of mathematics? In the mathematics classroom, especially at the high school level, virtually any sort of exercises in the subject can employ this strategy. It is, however, important to remember that this technique is less suitable for use as initial instruction on a topic, since the very use of the strategy presupposes some knowledge on the part of most of the students. Peer problem solving is much more successful when it is used as a strategy for practice after a concept has been taught, and as a method to diagnose and remediate any faulty thought processes that may remain.

Which students can benefit most by application of the technique? The strategy works equally well for remedial students (who especially need to experience success at solving problems) and for average and high-achieving students. For many students, this approach is something completely different from all the mathematics teaching to which they have hitherto been exposed, and, while they often begin their participation with some skepticism and uncertainty, they become enthusiastic supporters of the method after seeing how well it works.

How can students be grouped for best problem-solving results? Using a taxonometric approach (for which we drew upon the work of Bloom and others), we note that we can classify students on the basis of two variables: skill level and confidence.

Skill Level I: Basic understanding—defines, recalls, recognizes
Skill Level II: Solves, interprets, classifies
Skill Level III: Applies, estimates, explains, generalizes
Skill Level IV: Evaluates, appraises, selects, justifies, discusses

Confidence A: Low confidence—needs constant supervision and encouragement
Confidence B: Needs occasional supervision and assistance
Confidence C: Able to work independently, needs support in assisting others
Confidence D: High confidence, able to work independently and to assist others

When these variables are assembled into a two-dimensional structure, it becomes much easier to assess students' current positions in the class with an eye toward effective grouping. Note that some combinations simply do not occur often enough to be included (for instance, it would be rare indeed to find a student with the lowest skill level yet the highest confidence rating!).

A chart showing the various combinations can be found on the next page.

		CONFIDENCE				
	Least	A	B	C	D	Most
	I	X	X			
	II		X	X	X	
SKILL	III			X	X	
	IV			X	X	
	Most					

These criteria are indicators of what a student knows and how confident he or she is of knowing it, and are useful in determining the compositions and sizes of problem-solving groups in the classroom. The smaller the group, the closer the students' skill levels should be, and ideally, the wider the range of student confidence (recognizing the caveat that students with very low skill levels cannot usually help or stimulate each other very much, nor do they exhibit high levels of confidence). Students with high skill levels, when matched in pairs with low-skill-level students, often become impatient and do not feel stimulated or challenged. In larger groups, a wider range both of skill level and of confidence can be effective. Therefore, attention must be paid to composition of the group so that every student can be involved and stimulated by the activity.

Sizes of groups depend both on the problem assignment and on the amount of time available. Research has shown that sizes of groups can range from two to six students and still allow interaction among all members. Groups should be kept as small as possible in order to facilitate the maximum amount of interaction.

Because most mathematics assignments involve the checking of computation or the review of graphic or written material, students should be seated side-by-side rather than across from each other, to avoid the difficulty of having to read upside down. The teacher should take this consideration into account as well when groups are larger than two.

What sorts of activities work best using the peer problem-solving approach? The area of math that comes to mind is that of word, or story, problems. In fact, virtu-ally any sort of mathematics exercise which requires multiple steps, translation, or analysis lends itself well to application of peer problem solving. Students have always had difficulty in translating problems into algebraic expressions, writing (and then solving) formulas, writing inductive and deductive proofs, and in general applying skills they know to unfamiliar situations where some analysis is required. Involving the students in these processes through the problem-solving approach helps them immensely, since, because they are **forced** to analyze and explain the steps that they take in finding solutions, they are much better able to verbalize the concepts to others, thus developing a real feeling for the necessary thought processes as well as an ability to communicate these processes to others.

To be more specific, peer problem solving has been used successfully at all levels of high school mathematics, from pre-algebra to college algebra and pre-calculus. Classroom teachers find peer problem solving an excellent tool for corrective feedback, practice, and formative evaluation, since observation of the students and the way they involve themselves in the technique is of great value in making real-time adjustments to what is taught—and the way it is taught.

Here are some samples of types of mathematics exercises suitable for peer problem-solving applications. For each of the problems given, we have noted those characteristics of the solution process which make each of the problems good for use with the peer problem-solving strategy. The possibilities mentioned here merely scratch the surface.

1. **Pre-algebra**
   A mechanic earns $11 an hour.
   a) If he works 12 hours, find his total earnings.
   b) Find his wages for a 40-hour week.
   c) If he works **h** hours, write a formula for his wages, **w.**
   (Multi-step problem, requiring the student to develop an algorithm for solving the problem based on his experience, calculate solutions for more than one set of data, and generalize the process for similar problems, translating it into an algebraic expression.)

2. **Algebra**
   Solve the inequality. Also show the graph of the solution set:
   $$21-15a < -8a-7$$
   (Requires student to recall and apply rules for transforming inequality statements, then to translate the algebraic result into a pictorial representation. Also requires recognition and application of the fact that such problems almost always have a solution set containing more than one element.)

3. **Advanced Algebra**

The linear term of a quadratic equation was incorrectly copied by a student who made no other mistake. She found the roots of her equation to be 6 and -2. Another student made an error only in copying the constant term and found -5 and -3 as the roots. What were the roots of the original equation?

(Requires the student to know and apply the relations between roots and coefficients of a quadratic equation, to be able to apply the property of the sum and product of quadratic roots, to be able to work backwards from the apparent sets of results and compare the processes used in achieving them, in order to detect the error and correct it.)

4. **Geometry**

Prove that in a 30-60-90 degree triangle the ray which bisects the larger acute angle divides the opposite leg into segments with lengths in the ratio 1 to 2.

(Requires the student to demonstrate knowledge of definitions of terms used in the problem, knowledge of how to apply theorems relating similar right triangles, ability to select an appropriate procedure for proof, and ability to justify each step of that procedure in line with accepted standards for proofs.)

What is said and done by the participants in the process? It is important to remember that the actual steps and statements by the problem-solver, listener and teacher will probably vary. The actual statements are not important. What is important is that all are involved in the process and in active thinking. Let us look at the process as it might be applied to the first of our example problems:

PROBLEM SOLVER: (Reads the first question.)

"Well, if he works one hour, that's $11. So I ought to be able to add up $11 twelve times."

LISTENER: "That makes sense. But is that the only way you could solve it?"

PS: "Actually, I guess I could just multiply twelve times $11.

L: "Good! What do you get?"

PS: "132."

TEACHER: "Please rephrase that and give the full answer to the question, because '132' by itself is not enough."

PS: "His total earnings for twelve hours are $132."

L: "O.K.; now for question B."

PS: (Reads the second question.)

"Maybe I should multiply $11 times seven, and then multiply by forty."

L: "Why?"

PS: "Well, there's seven days in a week, and he works a forty-hour week."

L: "Better go back and re-read the question."

T:	"You might find it useful to count the number of hours he works in a week, first."
PS:	(Reads the second question again.)
	"Oh, I get it. He only works 40 hours all week!"
L:	"So, does the number of days matter?"
PS:	"No, I guess it doesn't!"
L:	"Right. So what comes next?"
PS:	"Multiply 40 times $11, and get. . .ah. . .$440."
L:	"Good. How do you answer the question?"
PS:	"His wages for a 40-hour week will total $440."
T:	"Is this a reasonable number?"
PS:	"Well, sure—because what he earns for 40 hours is a lot more than what he earns for 12 hours."
L:	"How much more?"
PS:	"Hmmm. . .more than three times as much—which works, because 40 is more than three times twelve."
L:	"I get it! Good explanation!"
T:	"Well done. That's called 'estimation,' by the way."
L:	"Let's finish it off now."
PS:	(Reads the last question.)
	"This ought to be easy, but they don't give any numbers!"
L:	"What DO you have?"
PS:	"Letters."
L:	"What are letters used for?"
PS:	"In place of numbers usually. Let me read it again." (Reads.)
	"Well, I guess he still earns $11 an hour."
L:	"How do you know that?"
PS:	"Because they didn't give a new amount for what he gets each hour."
L:	"Good. Please go on."
PS:	"So, I suppose this one is a multiplication problem just like the other two questions."
L:	"What are you going to multiply?"
PS:	"Let's see. Last time it was $11 times 40 hours, so I'll try $11 times (h) hours, even though I don't know what (h) is."
L:	"What about the (w)?"
PS:	"Looks like that will have to be the answer when I multiply."
L:	"O.K., so how would you write the whole formula?"
PS:	$11 times (h) equals (w)."
T:	"What's that formula good for?"
PS:	"Well, if you know how many hours the man works, you can just plug it into the formula and find out how much he makes."
T:	"That's a good idea!"
L:	"Let's do another one, but this time I want to be the problem solver."

Jacqueline H. Simmons is the principal of Paul Robeson High School in Chicago. Deberah E. Perkins and Timothy R. Colburn are teachers at the school. For further information on their program to teach analytical thinking skills and problem solving, contact:

Jacqueline H. Simmons, Ed.D.
Paul Robeson High School
6835 South Normal Boulevard
Chicago, IL 60621

REFERENCES

Whimbey, Arthur and Jack Lochhead. 1982. **Problem Solving and Comprehension.** Philadelphia: The Franklin Institute Press.

Johnson, David W. and Roger T. Johnson, Edythe Johnson Holubec, and Patricia Roy. 1984. **Circles of Learning: Cooperation in the Classroom.** Association for Supervision and Curriculum Development.

WORKING WITH "UNDERPREPARED" MATHEMATICS STUDENTS

by Arthur B. Powell

"I'm just wondering if this is a new method of teaching and are we guinea pigs?"

This was R's only journal entry for the second week of class. In their journals, other students commented on the problem-solving activities, on how difficult they thought it would be to maintain daily journals, or asked questions about the assigned research problem. In the face of such a comment, I too was wondering! Though his name was on the initial class roster, R started attending only after the first week of class; he mentioned something about having to make arrangements with his employer. Thus, he missed the few introductory remarks I gave during the second class meeting, and now he left this brief journal entry that left me wondering. Had he enjoyed his first week of classes? Was he indicating that he was going to change sections if the course did not change focus and begin to meet his expectations? What were his expectations and academic background?

At the age of 15, after intermittently attending his final year of junior high school, R never bothered to enter high school. He describes the experience of school up until then as emotionally devastating and irrelevant. He preferred the environment of his family's apartment in Newark's Columbus Homes—a twelve-story, semi-squalid, public housing complex with a third of its buildings' windows covered with plywood sheets—and he preferred working under age in factories to attending classes which seemed to have little connection to his life. After a while, the repetitious nature of factory work reminded him of school, and he decided to give school a second chance and obtained a high school equivalency diploma at 19. Later, he did a semester's stint at a community college and, at 21, entered the Newark College of Arts and Sciences at Rutgers University.

R is both typical and atypical of other students in development mathematics courses I teach. They tend to be younger, though R is not the oldest. The majority are female. Economic constraints of their families require many to have part-time jobs. Most students have completed high school but graduated with little proficiency in mathematics. Their relationships to mathematics, for one reason or another, has been a kind of progressive estrangement. They had come to believe, as R puts it, "that being able to understand mathematics was an in-born trait, like that of a concert pianist." Not to understand mathematics is to fear it and to lose confidence in oneself in relation to it.

Like thousands of others across the country, a large proportion of the students in these courses are accepted into the University under special admissions criteria. Over the years, however, an increasing number of so-called regularly admitted students are being placed into developmental mathematics courses. That is, R's mathematics "competence level" as he began the course was similar to that of many high school students. Consequently, I believe that my experiences with R and his peers are relevant to many high school teachers.

Euphemistically called "underprepared college students," this group of students was placed in the first of a two-course developmental mathematics sequence at Rutgers, based on the results of an in-house placement examination. These courses are designed to upgrade their performance so that they can go on to complete the mathematics proficiency requirement. I have taught these courses for a number of years. The one in which R enrolled was concerned primarily with numerical computation; fractions, decimals, percents, word problems, signed numbers, and some elementary algebra are topics prescribed in the curriculum. As I teach the course, departing from a traditional teaching mode, these topics as well as others are included. In this chapter, rather than enumerate the content and teaching approach of the course,[1] I will describe the following three pedagogical devices:

- journals
- creative writing and research problems
- explorations and problem-generating activities

First, however, it is important to set a philosophical context. Mathematics and the purpose of mathematics education, like any human enterprise, can be viewed in a multiplicity of ways. In one view, mathematics has been described as an intellectual or aesthetic activity whose truths are ordained and whose methods can only be practiced by a gifted intellectual elite, who are trained to contribute to the economic, political, technical, and military needs and ambitions of society.

Doing mathematics, on the other hand, can also be seen as a specific use of one's mental functionings, such as listening, observing, touching, abstracting, "imaging," classifying, and so on. These functionings are focused on studying patterns, attributes, and relationships of objects found in one's milieu and their dynamics. Mathematical meaning is constructed and is a by-product or outcome of one's conscious perception of and action on the objects. Pluckett suggests that doing mathematics also involves

> a lot of wondering "What if. . .?" and working out the consequences of hypotheses, checking for inconsistencies, proving results in such a way as to convince others. It very much depends upon using symbols and diagrams, to communicate with ourselves as much as with others as an aid to the convenient handling of ideas. (1981, p. 47)

In short, it is a human activity of the mind; one which involves feelings and requires the types of mental powers possessed by individuals capable of using their native language (Gattegno, 1971).

As one of its purposes, then, mathematical education could aim to assist learners in becoming aware of the powers they possess and how they can construct meaning and procedural know-how. It could empower learners with self-confidence, self-realization, and autonomous functioning in relation to mathematics while developing their competence.

For teachers, this view of mathematics and its educational aims requires that our teaching methods and approaches differ from conventional ones. It is fair to cite traditional methods of mathematics teaching employed in school—what Paulo Freire (1971) describes as the "banking method" of education—as a contributing factor to the presence of large numbers of students at the secondary and tertiary levels in remedial and developmental math courses. We have to search for ways to structure activities, lessons, and curricula which allow students to construct conceptual meaning of mathematical entities. (For further discussion of this point, see Confrey, 1981). In sum, we need to create situations in which our students are **active producers** rather than mere **passive repositories of knowledge.** It is toward this end that I use the three pedagogical devices.

Journals

The journal is one of the tools I use to have students reflect critically on their perceptions, conceptions, and actions. It is also used as a vehicle for them to express their feelings. Their journals provide a powerful way for me to "see" inside of them and as a means of private communications between us.

Each student is asked to make daily entries, or at least one for each class or assignment, into her or his journal. They may write on any of a number of topics, to be detailed subsequently. Because writing is considered a chore by many students, they are advised to write for only five minutes each time. This suggestion helps to relieve any anxiety concerning the amount of writing they are to produce. After becoming accustomed to the idea, most find themselves spending more than five minutes to express their thoughts.

I request that they write on 8½"×11" loose-leaf paper. Generally, one or two sheets are sufficient for a week's writing. It is emphasized that neither their grammar nor syntax is of concern, only what they have to say. When writing, they are to focus on **themselves:** what **they** have done, discovered, invented, or felt. They may write on any topic or issue they choose, but the following are questions offered to stimulate thought and reflection.

TEACHING MATHEMATICS

1. What did **you** do in class or on the assignment?

2. What did **you** learn from the class activities or assignments?

3. What questions do **you** have about the work **you** did or were not able to do?

4. Describe any discoveries **you** have made about mathematics or yourself.

5. What attributes, patterns, or relationships do **you** see?

6. How do **you** feel about **your** work, discoveries, the class or assignment?

7. What confused **you** today? What did **you** like? What did **you** not like?

8. Describe any computational procedure **you** have invented.

The previous week's journal entries are collected at the beginning of the week and returned by the end of the week with comments, which I attempt to make nonjudgmental, on the substance of what is written. When someone has written about a discovery, I might ask for an explanation or demonstration in class, or I might ask the student to write how he or she came to make the discovery.

The following are examples of the type of discoveries students have written about, quoted from their journals. The first is about an "invented" procedure made after some work with Cuisenaire rods to investigate factorization and common factors. No procedural techniques were given; class time had ended. Students were asked if they could develop a procedure for finding the greatest common factor of a set of integers. One student wrote:

> First you look at the prime factorization of each group of integers. Then you choose the exponents that are common within both groups of integers.
>
> e.g., $2^2 \times 3^1 = 12$ and $2^2 \times 3^2 = 36$.
> The greatest common factor is $2^2 \times 3^1 = 12$.

The second is an example of a student who is beginning to realize the usefulness of collaborative work in problem-solving situations.

> It was helpful to work with the individuals in my group because their ideas on the problem and also their ways of solving it help me a lot more. Listening to each other helped us to see the problem clearer.

Questions of all sorts appear in the journals. I may answer some directly. More often than not, I respond with a question to push their thinking further. At first, some students have a tendency to write journals which read like lesson plans.

> Today we looked for patterns in the extended multiplication table from worksheet #10. This was fun.

To which I would ask the student to describe the patterns that **she** found. After a while, students come to see the value of the journals as a reflective exercise; some even begin to comment philosophically. Some students who prefer to remain quiet in class make interesting points in their journals. The following is from one such student. Her comments relate to operating with fractions in a different base of numeration.

> While doing worksheets #42 and #43, I felt as if I had just learned how to count. It was pretty frustrating to keep using the addition and multiplication tables for every problem. Though frustrating, it makes me realize how much I have taken mathematical numbers for granted. Before I took this course, math was just numbers and memorized rules. I know this is going to sound strange, but even though I like and find math easier, I see it is as something more complex.

The journals provide a means for students to monitor their own learning and changes in their attitude toward mathematics. Those weeks in which students have actively participated in class or worked thoroughly on assignments are evidenced in what they write. If little work has been done, there is not much to write about. In this way, the journal is a powerful self-monitoring tool. Regular feedback, at times more comprehensive than what can be accomplished in classroom interaction, can come from the instructor's comments. The journal also provides instructors with feedback on the clarity of lessons, on which students have been reached by a particular activity, and so on. It establishes a dialogue between students and teachers.

Reflection can lead to critical thinking. I have noticed this at the end of the semester when I collect the entire journal from each student. Reading through the journals gives an indication of the growth of a student's critical thinking abilities. In addition, a high correlation exists between those whose algorithmic and problem-solving performance have improved and the extent of in-depth, reflective and descriptive writing which they develop over the semester.

Creative Writing and Research Problems

Creative writing is not generally thought of as an aspect of mathematics learning. Most times students are required to be uncreative; they are subjected continuously to a search for "the" right answer. If a student were to respond to a test with $36^{-1/2}$ (5^2+1) as an answer to $4/3+3$, he or she would probably be accused of being a show-off for not supplying the standard, simple answer. However, there ought to be a place for such responses, and they can be encouraged. As Father Fernando Cardenal has stated:

> Any education that merits the name must prepare people for freedom—to have opinions, to be critical, to transform their world.

There are a number of mathematical writing projects and activities which can be used to stimulate creative writing, to allow students to deviate from the standard. (See Gattegno and Hoffman, 1976). There are a variety of purposes I have found for these activities. They include:
- to stimulate self-expression in mathematics notation,
- to bring awareness of the multiple ways to express an idea,
- to de-emphasize a search for a single correct answer, and
- to focus on the use and practice of particular mathematical operations or objects (integers, rationals, and so on) in any base of numeration.

Particular activities can be structured to focus on any number of objectives. They can be used as a diagnostic technique. They can allow one to intervene at appropriate moments to work on students' misconceptions. Two examples I have found useful for this purpose are:

- Given a number (say .7), construct expressions equivalent to the number using multiplication, and
- Write expressions for integers from 1 to 35 (or 1 to 100) using, in each case, only the integers 1, 2, 3, and 4 and using each exactly once. Any operation or notation is permitted.

Some creative writing projects can be given as long-term assignments or "research problems." Research problems fall into two categories. The first comprises those situations which are new and undefined to the student and have finite outcomes that are already known to others. For example, what are all the composite numbers between 1 and 100? The second category contains problems which have infinite or indefinite or perhaps unreachable outcomes. An example is: "What is the largest fraction between 0 and 1?"

Working with "Underprepared" Mathematics Students

One example of a research problem arose from an in-class creative writing exercise. In the exercise, students were engaged in constructing different expressions for certain numbers given varying restrictions on allowable operations and numbers. From this work, the following question was posed.

Can you construct an expression for each number from 1 to 100 using the figure 4 exactly four times, and any operation?

This is a fairly well-known problem from the recreational mathematics literature, called "The Problem of the Four Fours" (see Graham, 1968, p. 27). Students were given a significant portion of the semester to work on this research problem, similar to a literature or history term paper.

Upon returning the students' papers, I also distribute a sheet which represents the collective efforts of the class. It has three sections: Runs—Exploiting an Idea, Interesting Individual Ideas, and Remaining Challenges. Examples of each for the class work on the Problem of the Four Fours:

I. Runs—Exploring an Idea

$$59 = \frac{4!}{.4} - \frac{4}{4}$$

$$60 = \frac{4!}{.4} \cdot \frac{4}{4}$$

$$61 = \frac{4!}{.4} + \frac{4}{4}$$

II. Interesting Individual Ideas

$$1 = \frac{\frac{\sqrt{4 \times 4}}{4}}{\sqrt{4}}$$

$$55 = \frac{4! - 4 + \sqrt{4}}{.4}$$

III. Remaining Challenges

73 and 87

There are many variations of this kind of research problem. Students enjoy exchanging ideas while working essentially on their own. One value of these activities was expressed in a student's journal. After the student reviewed his work and compared it to the sheet I distributed, he wrote:

> I was intrigued to see the unlimited variety of approaches that other students used to achieve the end product.... I began to see that reaching the desired result was not as interesting as the possibilities or possible ways of reaching it.

While studying how to find the decimal representation of fractions, some students took interest in their observation that for some fractions their decimal equivalent had a finite number of digits if appending an infinite number of zeros was disallowed, while others had an unending number of digits, though their pattern of digits was cyclical. I suggested that they research this observation further and report any results in their journals. The following is part of what L reported in her journal a week or so later.

> I investigated terminating decimals to find how it can be determined if a fraction's decimal expression will terminate and in how many decimal places it would terminate.

> I came to the conclusion that to determine if a fraction's decimal expression will terminate:
> a) Express it in its lowest terms and
> b) If 2 or 5, or 2 and 5 are the only prime factors, it will terminate.

> I also concluded that the number of places that the decimal will terminate in can be found in the prime factorization exponents. The number of the highest exponent corresponds with the number of places the decimal will terminate in.

L, a shy, reticent, and seemingly emotionless student, presented her findings to the class and then wrote the above statement with several examples. It is as succinct as the presentation she gave. She did, however, show signs of elation when she handed in this journal entry.

Explorations and Problem-Generating Activities

I incorporate problem-solving activities in the classroom so that students are producers rather than recipients of problems. Furthermore, the activities are based in part on the recognition that work on a problem "requires a passionate engagement of the person who would tackle it" (Wertime, 1979, p. 492). This caring about a nagging problem is what allows one to remain with it. If a challenge is too easy or too hard, if a student realizes that he or she is ill-equipped to handle it, then it will not be taken up. When a challenge has been accepted as a problem, it generates a kind of tension within the individual, a tension which is dissolved at the moment the problem is solved or dropped (Gattegno, et al, 1981).

How can we get our students passionately involved in a challenge to the extent that it creates tension in them? I have attempted to answer this by turning the question around: What types of situations can we present to students from which they can generate their **own** problems? In this way, students become the producers of problems about which we can presume they care. Working in this framework, the guidelines I use include the following:

- Present situations which can be mathematized or to which mathematical questions can be reasonably asked.
- Invite students to understand the situation and its mathematical possibilities by asking questions of it. (That is, they are encouraged to "enter into a dialogue" with the situation.)
- Ask students to pursue their questions and make refinements in some, generate new questions as old ones are answered, suspended, or made simpler.
- Remain open to considering questions not previously asked, or ones they have not fully explored.
- Pose questions to students to further their thinking on their questions or problems, or to have them consider their problems from a different point of view.
- Introduce new mathematical techniques, ways of organizing and analyzing data, and so on as students demonstrate a need for these.
- Maintain a classroom atmosphere which fosters and encourages students to exchange insights, findings, questions, points of view, and so on.

Students need time for **exploration** of a given situation during which they attempt to understand the situation and to observe patterns and relationships. **Problem-generating** occurs when they begin to ask questions concerning their observations. Once they compel themselves to engage in a process to find answers to their questions, they switch into a problem-solving mode.

There is a range of questions that they can ask, not all of which are mathematical ones, and techniques for generating questions. One of these is to pose "What if. . .?" questions concerning attributes of the situation. (Some educators call this the "What if not. . .?" technique. For a fuller discussion of this problem-posing technique, see Brown and Walter, 1983.)

A situation which can be structured into an exploration for students to engage in problem-generating is the 3X+1 Problem, also known as Ulam's Conjecture. (For further discussion, see Haynes, 1984.) It can be stated as follows:

> Choose any positive integer and call it N. If the number is even, divide it by 2, or in other words replace N by N/2. If the number is odd, triple it and add 1. In either case, the result is a new value of N.

Repeat this procedure on the new value of N and see what happens. Do this several times.

What do you notice?
What questions come to mind about this situation?

When I have used this exploration, a host of questions have been generated. A sampling of them are below.

1. Is it true that all positive integers will converge to 1? (This one is Ulam's conjecture in the form of a question.)
2. Will all sequences have the pattern $16 \rightarrow 8 \rightarrow 4 \rightarrow 2 \rightarrow 1$?
3. Will odd numbers require more steps to reach 1 than even numbers?
4. Can it be determined how many applications of the procedure are required to reach 1 for a given number?
5. What is the maximum value a given N attains in its sequence toward 1? Are these peak values special?
6. Can this be investigated on a computer?
7. Can two consecutive values of N take the same number of iterations to reach 1 and have the same maximum value?

Some results that students have arrived at:

*   If $N=2^n$, where n is a positive integer, then the number of iterations required to reach 1 is n, and N is the maximum value attained in the process.

*   Peak values for any initial N must be an even number.

*   If N is such that $3N+1=2^n$, where n is a positive integer, then the number of iterations required to reach 1 is n+1, and $3N+1$ is the maximum value attained in the process.

Conclusion

I have attempted to indicate the types of activities one can use to enliven the standard affairs in mathematics classrooms. I have also tried to demonstrate that students who are generally not considered capable of generating creative and insightful mathematics can be reached by these activities.

Many students in mathematics classes do not spontaneously and publicly ask questions which focus on understanding asserted facts—privately and among friends they may do so. This may be due to the pace of our assignments and modes of testing; they force students into memorizing end results to keep up.

Thus, an important ingredient in the kind of experience I have described is that the classroom atmosphere should not be rigid or authoritarian. The teacher must try to remove herself or himself, as much as possible, from the center of things.

From evidence gathered in my classroom, I am convinced that so-called "underprepared" students are quite prepared and anxious to learn, to negotiate meaning, and to understand mathematics. This is true in spite of their anxieties and use of avoidance strategies to save their egos. Teachers have options other than merely to cover the syllabus and thus to encourage mere memorization as the means to successful learning, both of which keep students from understanding the genesis of ideas and engender frustrations and anxieties in students. If teachers take advantage of those options, then the work of L and the others quoted above can become the rule rather than the exception.

Arthur B. Powell is Assistant Professor of Mathematics at Rutgers University. For further information on his strategies for working with "underprepared" students, contact:

Arthur B. Powell
Academic Foundations Department
Rutgers University
Newark, NJ 07102

NOTE

1. A forthcoming textbook, **Explorations in Basic Mathematics: Computation Through an Awareness of Algebra,** and instructor's manual by the author and Martin R. Hoffman can be referred to for details of the course.

REFERENCES

Brown, S.I. and M.I. Walter. 1983. **The Art of Problem Posing.** Philadelphia: The Franklin Institute Press.

Cardenal, Father Fernando. 1983. As quoted in: **And Also Teach Them to Read** by S. Hirshon with J. Butler, Connecticut: Lawrence Hill, p. 83.

Confrey, J. 1981. "Concepts, Processes and Mathematics Instruction." **For the Learning of Mathematics:** 2(3), 8-12.

Freire, P. 1971. **Pedagogy of the Oppressed.** New York: Herder and Herder.

Gattegno, C. 1971. **What We Owe Children: The Subordination of Teaching to Learning.** New York: Avon Books.

Gattegno, C. and M.R. Hoffman. 1976. **Handbook of Activities for the Teaching of Mathematics at the Elementary School.** New York: Human Education Inc.

Gattegno, C., A. Powell, S. Shuller, and D. Tahta. 1981. "A Seminar on Problem Solving." A communication in **For the Learning of Mathematics:** 2(1), 42-46.

Graham, L.A. 1968. **The Surprise Attack in Mathematics Problems.** New York: Dover Publications, p. 27.

Haynes, B. January 1984. "On the Ups and Downs of Hailstone Numbers: Computer Recreation," **Scientific American.**

Plunkett, S. 1981. "Fundamental Questions for Teachers." **For the Learning of Mathematics:** 2(2), 46-48.

Wertime, R. 1979. "Students, Problems, and 'Courage Spans' " in **Cognitive Process in Instruction,** ed. J. Lochhead and J. Clement. Philadelphia: The Franklin Institute Press, p. 192.